Finally The TRUTH Comes Out

Sean Williams

ISBN: 978-0-578-03199-6

Hello to you my friend. My physical name is Sean Williams. I say my "physical name" because that is the name that my physical mother and physical father decided to call me at the time which I came into the physical world. I have come to understand what it means to be in the physical world through many hours of meditation beyond the gates of consciousness and hope to pass this knowledge unto you. The most important thing to understand is: We are all God's children! You either realize it or you don't.

Have you ever really thought about religion? The so-called "organized" religions of the world rely on so-called "holy" books to teach their beliefs, but they do it in a dead language that is confusing for most people who attempt to understand it. Why would they make it confusing? They make it confusing so that you become frustrated and consistently return to them for guidance, all the while they hold the collection plate out. It is simply greed!

What they never tell you is, that there *IS* an easy way to understand the true spiritual messages within religion, and spirituality in general and also the teachings which Jesus taught, but in order for you to understand the meanings of his parables, you must first use the true keys of knowledge to unlock and open your spiritual mind.

The truth is that God did not deem the fruit of knowledge "forbidden". The devil's minions did that! In fact God created the fruit of knowledge specifically to empower our spiritual minds and show us the way to regain our spiritual consciousness. The one true God, the one who loves us unconditionally has only one goal, and that is to bring all of his children (us) home. "Home", simply being, back to spiritual consciousness. He designed the fruit of knowledge specifically to show us that we are his children and how to get home. If we go through our entire physical lives without ever establishing ourselves on the spiritual level (find heaven), then when it comes time for our physical lives to end, we won't know where to go. This is what Jesus meant when in the Gospel of Thomas saying #60 he was quoted as saying "seek for yourselves a place for rest, so you will not become a corpse and be eaten".

In this world, (the physical world) we are all spiritually unconscious. Spiritual unconsciousness is hell! God gave us the fruit of knowledge to show us how to get out of hell and the devil and his minions have fought to keep us confused and blind to this truth. They remain comfortable as long as they keep us from learning the truth. With this book I hope to put an end to their comfort!

This is the battle between God and the Devil and it goes on to this very day. There is a spiritual tug-of-war going on for each and every one of our very souls and it is up to each one of us to choose who we want to win. The Devils method is to try and convince us that we are not in hell, that physical consciousness is the only consciousness and keep us focused on trying to stay physically happy and comfortable so that we remain ignorantly consumed (trapped) by our physical path. As long as he keeps us focused on money, sex, food, partying, TV, sports, politics, or basically anything else that we enjoy about the physical world, we are not focused on our one true goal, returning to heaven (spiritual consciousness). The devil doesn't want you to know that death is not the end. As long as you fear death, you simply fear returning to heaven and God. He wins.

God's method is to try and keep us from being so happy in the physical world so that when the time comes for us to leave; we don't still desire to remain here. Death is not the end. It is simply the end of one consciousness and the beginning of another. If at the time of your physical death, you still desire to remain physically "alive" then you will not regain spiritual consciousness and you will be reborn into another physical body and forced to endure another "life" sentence in purgatory (some people believe you will not come back, but be consumed by the devil. Either way, it's not a good thing!). This is why he created the fruit of knowledge. He created it to show us that there is something waiting for us after this world so that we don't become so attached to "the world" that we are afraid to leave when our time comes. That is the "knowledge" that the fruit of knowledge endows us with.

Remember he loves us very much and his only goal is to help us not become so attached to the world that we decide to stay. If one never realizes that there is a better way of life waiting for them, they will just stay where they are and try and make the best out of it. That is how the devil fights God. The devil tries constantly to prevent us from focusing on the better way of life "out there" by constantly stimulating us here. In the physical world we are constantly bombarded with temporary stimulus which keeps us physically focused. Only once we are able to block out that temporary stimulus (positive and negative) will we be able to focus on the path of permanent happiness, spiritual happiness. Some people call this enlightenment, nirvana or God. I call it regaining spiritual consciousness.

In this book, I intend to cover three topics.

1. The cover-up of the truth about the fruit of knowledge.
2. The truth about Jesus' teachings being psychedelically induced. The Gospel of Thomas (which is Jesus' direct teachings) once decoded shows a way to understand the spirituality of a psychedelic experience in the physical mind, and ultimately leads those who understand it back to spiritual consciousness (heaven).
3. How to grow your own "manna" so that you too can put on "the mind of Christ" and begin the path back to spiritual consciousness.

Remember, we are all in hell right now, because in this world we are all distant from God in the way an unconscious person is distant from his conscious friends and family. The devil and his minions seek to keep us here in this condition and they have gone to great lengths to try and keep what I'm telling you secret. "Manna" is the antidote for our unconscious spiritual condition and yet it has been deemed "forbidden" by a church that doesn't want you to understand the truth so they don't lose their power or cash flow and also deemed "illegal" by a government that doesn't want to lose their control or their cash flow. The Church and Government are nothing more than the devil and his minions. Once this information becomes known and everyone begins to grow their own "manna" the devil will lose control and the rapture (mass transcendence) will take place in which everyone who has experienced the "keys of knowledge" will "wake up" in heaven (regain spiritual consciousness). It is up to each one of us to defeat the devil and our battle is our own. We must all save ourselves and we begin the road to salvation by eating the fruit of knowledge.

I wrote two other books but they include full color pictures and were quite extensive and therefore ended up being expensive, so with this book I'm going to keep the cost down by only making the covers color and simply indicating the proper topics for you to research so you may also see what I've seen.

The truth is: I cannot save you! But I can help you along on your own path to salvation. Ultimately it is up to you to save yourself. Your entire life is a test of whether or not you will surrender your life to God. We have all been poisoned with selfish physical desire (the desire to "live" physically) and we must all choose to let go of that selfishness. I can only give you the tools to prepare you to take your test. I cannot take your test for you. Sean Williams

The simplest way I can describe our task to you is: God infused his love into the psilocybe cubensis mushroom. His love will conquer the evil (ego and self) which the devil has poisoned each one of us with. We must all eat the psilocybin mushrooms. Once we eat them and begin to understand the truth, we need to encourage others to do the same. To work tirelessly towards the goal of helping others experience God's love firsthand through the use of mushrooms is to become a child of God (the Christ). This is why I've written this book. It is my goal to help God complete his will. We must not fail!

CHAPTER 1: THE COVER-UP OF THE FRUIT OF KNOWLEDGE

The true fruit of knowledge was not an apple! It was and still is a psilocybin mushroom! I have no reason to lie! I can only tell you the truth as I have come to understand it. I cannot make you believe it as truth. What you believe is entirely up to you and all I hope is that you don't believe simply what you are told to believe. Do your own research. Test my theory, and grow your spiritual knowledge. It is much easier to believe something that you yourself have experienced first-hand!

Since before the birth of "the church" and "organized" religion, many ancient cultures used visionary plants and potions to gain a better connection to God. The human species according to scientists has existed for 110,000 years. According to the bible, man has existed on earth for 6,000 years. Only since the creation of "The Bible" (new testament) in the last 1,900 years, has there been such a thing as a "forbidden" fruit. If you trace any religion back to its founder, eventually you will find a profound mystic.

The Wikipedia definition of mysticism:

"Mysticism (from the Greek, "mystikos", an initiate of a mystery religion) is the pursuit of communion with, identify with, or conscious awareness of an ultimate reality, divinity, spiritual truth, or God through direct experience, intuition, or insight. Mysticism usually centers on a practice or practices intended to nurture that experience or awareness."

The use of magic mushrooms is that very same mystical practice!

I said it before, and I'll say it again, it wasn't God who deemed the fruit of knowledge "forbidden". God actually wants us to eat it! It's the Devil who doesn't want us to eat the fruit because he feeds off of our spiritual energy, and his minions ("the church" and the federal government) are in charge of preventing the truth about the fruit of knowledge from coming out. If everyone awakens their spiritual consciousnesses and therefore complete their physical life journey back to spiritual consciousness, the devil will run out of food!

Jesus knew about the power of the fruit of knowledge and he devoted his life to teaching others about what he learned from this amazingly powerful fruit. He was teaching people to use the fruit of knowledge to find his father's kingdom within themselves and the Pharisees (the church, organized religious leaders) killed him for it.

What knowledge does the fruit of knowledge give those who eat it? The simplest answer is: The fruit of knowledge opens the gates of consciousness within your mind in order to allow you to temporarily experience what it feels like to regain your spiritual consciousness. It allows you temporary passage to heaven to prepare you for the ending of your physical consciousness.

Upon the end of your "physical" life (consciousness), if you have never experienced your spiritual consciousness, you will not know how to let go of the physical world. Since at that point you know nothing other than the physical world, that is where you will long to stay, and you will be reborn into another temporary physical body to live another temporary "physical" life with the hope of finally getting over the desire to have a physical life.

The true fruit of knowledge is the psilocybin mushroom, but the knowledge that it passes to those who eat it has become known as the psychedelic experience. The simplest way I can describe the psychedelic experience is a spiritual experience. Look up psychedelic experience on the Wikipedia specifically "the five levels" and you will see for yourself that many people have experienced religious phenomena at the higher levels. Through the Gospel of Thomas it is easy to see that Jesus himself also had his own psychedelic experience which greatly influenced his teachings (I will get more into this later).

The truth is the "church" deemed it forbidden because it allowed those who eat it to have their own personal intimate experience with God and the church wants their followers to believe that the only way to heaven and God's kingdom is through the church.

The simple truth about the psilocybin mushroom being created by God with sole the purpose of reuniting his children with him by the fusing of his love into the sacred mushroom is possibly the most important (re)discovery of the modern world. To deny this truth is to prevent yourself and others from experiencing God's love. I can definitely say that realizing this very fact has indeed changed my life for the better (even though the task of overcoming the deceptions that the church has brainwashed the people of the world with can feel incredibly overwhelming at times).

Jesus' teachings of the "keys of knowledge" (so he called them) were so powerful and easy for people to understand, that the church couldn't completely erase them, so they changed the image of them to an apple and told everyone that the devil created them to scare people away from trying to find the truth. By hiding the truth about the fruit of knowledge from the people of the world, they effectively trapped us all here and secured their own comfort.

During the "last supper", Jesus supposedly passed out bread and water which he turned to wine according to "the church", but then he also said, "Eat this in remembrance of me, for it is my flesh and drink this for it is my blood". The Aztecs called the psilocybin mushroom the "flesh of the gods" and it was greatly revered for its spiritual properties. This is not a coincidence! Tea can also be made from the psilocybin (magic) mushroom by simply mixing mushrooms in water with very little effort. Both eating mushrooms and drinking mushroom tea creates an intoxicating effect that is very similar to alcoholic intoxication except alcohol doesn't trigger an opening of the mind. This is the very reason the "last supper" meal of Jesus was changed to bread and wine. It's because they are hiding the truth from us to protect their comfort and cash flow. They have substituted a dried cracker and some grape juice to symbolize their lie so they don't lose control! They have substituted one intoxicating substance which doesn't open your spiritual mind for the original one that did!

Pure psilocybin mushrooms grown on sterilized substrate are not dangerous. Look it up on the internet! There has never been a proven death from overdose from eating psilocybin cubensis (magic) mushrooms. In fact they have been proven to be less toxic to the body than aspirin or a cigarette. The biggest danger of eating magic mushrooms is the occurrence of what has become known as "a bad trip". A bad trip is simply becoming afraid as the gates of consciousness begin to open and one begins to feel the unknown spiritual consciousness. This fear can become overwhelming to some and ultimately is the final true obstacle standing in front of any who seek spiritual enlightenment. They are definitely not deadly and it is of the highest importance that you yourself test this theory and see for yourself if what I'm saying is true. Remember, whatever doesn't kill you, only makes you stronger.

In the story of Moses, God sent down "Manna" from heaven to feed Moses and the exiles while on their pilgrimage through the wilderness. The translation of the term "wilderness" is "pasture" where livestock graze. Psilocybin mushrooms grow naturally from cattle, horse, sheep, elephant, and other animal dung and Moses and the exiles carried a great number of livestock with them on their journey. "Manna" was found with the morning dew. These are the exact conditions for psilocybin mushrooms to grow! Make the connection! This makes sense!

This is taken from the Wikipedia reference on "manna":

"The origin of "Manna" is clearly in heaven according to the Bible (Psalms 78:24,25, Psalm 105:40 and John 6:31), but the various naturalistic identifications of "manna" have been compared to things in nature. In the Mishnah "manna" is treated as a supernatural substance, created during the twilight of the first Friday in existence, and ensured to be clean by the sweeping of the ground by a northern wind, and subsequent rains, before it arrives. According to classical rabbinical literature, "manna" was ground in a heavenly mill for the use of the righteous, but some of it was allocated to the wicked and left for them to grind themselves."

"In the description in the Book of Exodus, "manna" is described as being available each morning after the dew had evaporated. It is described in the Book of Numbers as arriving with the dew during the night; the Book of Exodus adds that "manna" was comparable to hoarfrost in size, and similarly had to be collected before it was melted by the heat of the sun. According to the Book of Exodus in the Bible, "Manna" is described as being white "like coriander seed" in color. The book of Numbers describes it as having the appearance of bdellium."

This is the direct passage taken from the book of Exodus in the Bible:

"Then said the LORD unto Moses, Behold, I will vain bread from heaven for you; and the people shall go out and gather a certain rate every day, that I may prove them, whether they will walk in my law or no (16:4). And when the dew that lay was gone up, behold, upon the face of the wilderness there lay a small round thing, as small as the hoar frost on the ground (16:14). And when the children of Israel saw it, they said one to another, It is manna: for they knewist not what it was. And Moses said unto them, this is the bread which the Lord hath given you to eat."

I can go on and on about the similarities of the biblical descriptions of "Manna" to the psilocybin mushroom, but for expense purposes I will keep it short. Look at the pictures on the cover of the book to see for yourself how similar a psilocybin mushroom is to the features attributed to "manna" and the similarities will be undeniable, then once you eat a small amount, you will know in your heart and soul that what I'm saying is true.

For further research, use the internet to lookup, Psychedelic experience, near death experience, and mysticism on the Wikipedia. The similarities are no coincidence!

CHAPTER 2:
THE TRUE MEANINGS OF THE GOSPEL OF THOMAS

The Gospel of Thomas is a map to guide us to find the magic mushroom and find the true magic of the mushroom which is the path back to heaven and spiritual consciousness through the psychedelic experience.

First thing you must understand is that "organized" religion has most of the people of "the world" brainwashed into thinking any gospel other than the four included in the bible (canonical) are heretical. The thing about "heresy" is it refers to any belief that did not fit with what the church was teaching. Jesus himself was deemed a "heretic" before he was put to death by the Church. The church crucified Jesus for what he believed in and what he was teaching others. Their deception is so powerful that the church has everyone celebrating the fact that they killed the messiah by wearing cross pendants around their necks and worshiping a cross on which they crucified him. It was common practice for the church to kill "heretics" in the name of God. I guess "Thou shalt not kill!" doesn't apply to them? Don't celebrate Jesus' death. Celebrate his life by studying and understanding his teachings and using them to wake up, which is what he wants. He only wants us all to wake up.

Therefore I would also be deemed a "heretic" for what I'm telling you. I thank God that we finally have religious freedom so that I can finally finish the work that Jesus began without anyone silencing me before my work is complete. Even if they did kill me as they did Jesus, they wouldn't take anything from me that I'd be afraid to lose, because I know what I'm doing is right, and I've seen the world beyond this one and long to return there. But I will not go until my promise to God is fulfilled.

THE GOSPEL OF THOMAS

The Gospel of Thomas is a collection of sayings (parables) that the living Jesus spoke and Didymos Judas Thomas recorded. Every saying in this document has psychedelic meaning.

1. And he said, "Whoever discovers the interpretation of these sayings will not taste death."

In this statement he tells everyone who reads this document the importance of finding the true meanings of these sayings. Understand that the "hidden" meaning of these sayings relates to using psilocybin mushrooms to overcome the fear of death. The psychedelic experience from the psilocybin mushroom being a temporary "near death experience" which reveals that death is not the end but merely a transition from one consciousness to the next takes away the fear of death. To fear death is to taste death. Once you've experienced the end of your physical consciousness temporarily, when it comes for you permanently will be no big deal. Therefore you will not taste it because you will understand that you will be merely "waking up" in heaven and not actually dying.

2. Jesus said, "Those who seek should not stop seeking until they find. When they find, they will be disturbed. When they are disturbed, they will marvel, and will reign over all. [and after they have reigned they will rest.]" *This statement is a direct relation to the psychedelic experience achieved through the use of the magic mushroom. Jesus was encouraging his followers to push past their fear and achieve a level 5 psychedelic experience in which "those who seek" find God. When you eat magic mushrooms you are "seeking". The first time you eat a heavy dose (3.5 dried grams or above) it can be a terrifying (disturbing) experience. Once you overcome the fear, that is when the WOW! Happens (you will marvel). Once you achieve a complete connection to God, you will be strong against the negativity of the world (reign over all).You will realize that it takes great effort to remain in the physical world and you will look forward to the end of your time here (you will rest)*

3. Jesus said, "If your leaders say to you, 'Look, the (Father's) kingdom is in the sky,' then the birds of the sky will precede you. If they say to you, 'It is in the sea,' then the fish will precede you. Rather, the (Father's) kingdom is within you and it is outside you.

When you know yourselves, then you will be known, and you will understand that you are children of the living Father. But if you do not know yourselves, then you live in poverty, and you are the poverty." *This saying refers to how the leaders of organized religion mislead their followers by saying heaven is in the sky instead of teaching the path of* *introspective meditation through the use of the keys of knowledge (magic mushrooms). When you use magic mushrooms and have a level 5 experience, some see it as finding your true self (the "awakened" spiritual you). Jesus prized spiritual wealth (spiritual knowledge and experience) over physical wealth. If you never try magic mushrooms, then you will never come to know your true self and you will be spiritually lacking (living in spiritual poverty). To be spiritually awakened is to know yourself, and you are spiritually wealthy.*

4. Jesus said, "The person old in days won't hesitate to ask a little child seven days old about the place of life, and that person will live.

For many of the first will be last, and will become a single one."

This refers to rebirth and how an old person locks away spiritual knowledge to focus on the physical path. A child seven days old will still have their spiritual goal in mind, whereas the old adult will desire their spiritual goal but due to a life of being focused on their physical path, will have forgotten how to reach it. This is what the magic mushroom teaches. A magic mushroom also becomes fully grown within seven days.

5. Jesus said, "Know what is in front of your face, and what is hidden from you will be disclosed to you.

For there is nothing hidden that will not be revealed. [And there is nothing buried that will not be raised.]" *The meaning of this statement is, understanding the knowledge achieved during the psychedelic experience. Knowing what is in front of your face, is knowing that the world in front of our face is an illusion of our unconscious spiritual self. Many people experience "static" and auras, or swirling lines around lights and reflections of the sun after frequent use of psychedelic mushrooms. This is nothing more than the pixels of the illusion. They were there the whole time; you just didn't know how to see them before the manna awakened your spiritual self and allowed you to see with your spiritual eye. Before the psychedelic experience your physical self filtered out and dismissed those distortions in the illusion because it didn't understand them as they were. Our entire physical lives are our "judgment" and we are being watched. Don't do anything you don't want to answer for. Know that magic mushrooms are the keys to awakening your spiritual self.*

6. His disciples asked him and said to him, "Do you want us to fast? How do you want us to pray? Should we give to charity? What diet should we observe?"

Jesus said, "Don't lie, and don't do what you hate, because all things are disclosed before heaven. After all, there is nothing hidden that will not be revealed, and there is nothing covered up that will remain undisclosed". *This statement refers to the judgment which you begin to understand as you consume the "manna" (magic mushrooms). Magic mushrooms make your understanding of the difference between your spiritual path and physical path clearly defined. Fasting, giving to charity and diet are all physical concerns. Praying is pointless. Jesus talked to them on the spiritual level. He told them to always remain focused on the end, and only to do things you will be happy that you did, not ashamed. Magic mushrooms prove whether or not you are willing to surrender your life to God. To understand this opens the gates of heaven for you. Focus on God's will regardless of what happens to you. Selfless love and devotion is what God wants. To look back at your life in the end and remember giving your life to God, now that, my friends, is a spiritual treasure.*

7. Jesus said, "Lucky is the lion that the human will eat, so that the lion becomes human. And foul is the human that the lion will eat, and the lion still will become human." *This statement has been said other ways, "you are what you eat". Remember that magic mushrooms are spiritual medicine and to be purely human is to be impurely physical (foul). Use the "manna" to become a spiritual person instead of a physical person and you will become "enlightened".*

8. And he said, "The person is like a wise fisherman who cast his net into the sea and drew it up from the sea full of little fish. Among them the wise fisherman discovered a fine large fish. He threw all the little fish back into the sea, and easily chose the large fish. Anyone here with two good ears had better listen!" *This statement refers to becoming the "large fish" through spiritual growth by using the "manna" (keys of knowledge) as Jesus did. In the physical world due to the intentional misdirection by the "church" (Pharisees) we have all been kept as "little fish" (they deemed the fruit of knowledge- "forbidden"). The magic mushrooms are spiritual food and in order to grow you must eat. Eat magic mushrooms and grow your spirit, so that when the time comes for you to leave the "world" you are not returned because you are still just a "little fish".*

9. Jesus said, "Look, the sower went out, took a handful (of seeds), and scattered (them). Some fell on the road, and they didn't take root in the soil and didn't produce heads of grain. Others fell on Thorns,

and they choked the seeds and worms ate them. And others fell on good soil, and it produced a good crop: it yielded sixty per measure and one hundred twenty per measure". *This refers to people who are suited to become disciples, the "seed" represents his teaching about the truth of the keys of knowledge being magic mushrooms, (God's will being to wake everyone up) and where they fell, represented the people he taught, whether or not they accepted his teachings and spiritually grew from them. He of course is "the sower". When the seed fell on the "road" or the "thorns" he was speaking of telling the truth about the magic mushrooms to a "closed" minded person who was unwilling to learn.*

I too have now cast the seeds of truth upon you, what will you do now? Will you dismiss them or will you allow them to take root and grow. You need to eat magic mushrooms!

10. Jesus said, "I have cast fire upon the world, and look, I'm guarding it until it blazes".

This refers to his intention to spread the truth (the world being our prison which keeps us by our own choice) about the keys of knowledge's true purpose in the world. Its' purpose being to undo the bonds which bind us to "the world" by giving us the "knowledge" that we are all actually spiritually unconscious. They provide the knowledge that there is a better life waiting for us once we learn how to make the choice to "let go" of our physical lives, and its' ability to bring all of God's unconscious spirits back to consciousness.

11. Jesus said, "This heaven will pass away, and the one above it will pass away.

The dead are not alive, and the living will not die. During the days when you ate what is dead, you made it come alive. When you are in the light, what will you do? On the day when you were one, you became two. But when you become two, what will you do?"

This refers to the idea of this world being similar to heaven, except as a negatively poisoned one which is quarantined distantly from the real heaven, with a spiritual unconscious "ward" where we are all "sleeping or unconscious", just outside of the gates to the real heaven. Once we are all cured of our unconscious states, then there will be no more "world", or the necessity for the "ward" in-between this world and heaven. It also references the light (the spirit world), and how your one spiritual consciousness separated when it became unconscious and then that consciousness came into the physical world. Will you focus your entire life on your physical path, or will you decide to not follow the physical path and instead focus on your spiritual path. Once you use the magic mushrooms to become spiritually awakened, will you try and help others to find their spiritual path as Jesus did?

12. The disciples said to Jesus, "We know that you are going to leave us. Who will be our leader?

Jesus said to them, "No matter where you are, you are to go to James the Just, for whose sake heaven and earth came into being". *This refers to his teachings of the fruit of knowledge causing their spirits to grow enough so that they can look inside themselves for guidance. If they can go to James the Just, no matter where they are, then James the Just must be inside of them as a spirit guide. Referring to Transcendence/meditation which magic mushrooms trigger.*

13. Jesus said to his disciples, "Compare me to something and tell me what I am like".

Simon Peter said to him, "You are like a just messenger".

Matthew said to him, "You are like a wise philosopher".

Thomas said to him, "Teacher, my mouth is utterly unable to say what you are like."

Jesus said, "I am not your teacher. Because you have drunk, you have become intoxicated from the bubbling spring that I have tended."

And he took him and withdrew, and spoke three sayings to him. When Thomas came back to his friends they asked him, "What did Jesus say to you?"

Thomas said to them, "If I tell you one of the sayings he spoke to me, you will pick up rocks and stone me, and fire will come from the rocks and devour you.

This refers to him wanting to know how his disciples saw him, he wanted to reinforce that he was not their teacher, he was just a guide helping them to see what was already around them the whole time, signs put there by the true teacher, God. The sayings he spoke were the Gnostic secrets about this world being created as a trap, and death was the only permanent way out of it, but only once you are spiritually ready (spiritually grown through the use of magic mushrooms) will you transcend back to permanent spiritual consciousness. He probably told Thomas about how he came to be as wise as he was, by eating the fruit of knowledge, and how others were not ready for that knowledge, and they would dispute the truth even if he told them.

14. Jesus said to them, "If you fast, you will bring sin upon yourselves, and if you pray, you will be condemned, and if you give to charity, you will harm your spirits.

When you go into any religion and walk about in the country side, when people take you in, eat what they serve you and heal the sick among them.

After all, what goes into your mouth will not defile you; rather, it's what comes out of your mouth that will defile you"

This refers to putting too much emphasis on physical actions, which also becomes understood upon consuming psychedelic mushrooms. By fasting you will become hungry, and you are more likely to give in to temptation (distracted by physical desire) and eat impure things (as in meat). By giving to charity, you are simply spreading physical entanglements to others who have been gifted poor by God. Remember Jesus favored the poor. He felt that the poor (uncomfortable) were better suited to leave the "world" than the rich (comfortable). By praying for physical things you are walking the physical path. True prayer is focusing on how you can help God awaken all of his unconscious children. Ask God for only what you need to fulfill that goal. Heal the "sick" (the ones confused by the deceptions of the church) among them by teaching them the simple truth. By refusing food to someone who offers it to you, you might offend them and thus send them down the physical path of anger. If you've learned the truth about the fruit of knowledge and then hide it, as the Pharisees have done, you will be defiled. Instead, tell the world the truth. Scream it from your roof tops or find some other way to get the message out.

15. Jesus said, "When you see one who was not born of woman, fall on your faces and worship. That one is your Father." *This refers to one outside of the physical world (a purely spiritual being a.k.a. God), because to be in the physical world is to be born of woman. Yes, he was also born of woman! He was saying don't worship him! The understanding of the difference between the spiritual world and the physical world is common after a level 4-5 psychedelic mushroom experience. Also,* *mushrooms are not "born" of woman, they come from spores.*

16. Jesus said, "Perhaps people think that I have come to cast peace upon the world. They do not know that I have come to cast conflicts upon the earth: fire, sword, war.

For there will be five in a house: there'll be three against two and two against three, father against son and son against father, and they will stand alone." *This refers to the war in heaven in which this "world" was the result; it was his goal to help God undo this "world" by guiding us all out of our unconscious states, which is understood after eating the fruit of knowledge, and having a psychedelic experience. His teachings were so powerful that one may become ostracized by his brainwashed (by the Pharisees) family after becoming spiritually conscious and then trying to guide others. It also refers to us all being "alone" in this world, regardless of "family", friends, or any other relationship attachments. One physical body cannot merge into another, and thus we are all spiritually alone inside of our physical bodies).*

17. Jesus said, "I will give you what no eye has seen, what no ear has heard, what no hand has touched, what has not arisen in the human heart." *This refers to spiritual truth, or God, because eye, ear, hand and even the human heart are all physical things, and spiritual truth, like God, is not physical. The psychedelic experience is not physical. It is spiritual. This is a blatant reference to the psychedelic experience achieved through the use of magic mushrooms.*

18. The disciples said to Jesus, "Tell us, how our end will come?"

Jesus said, "Have you found the beginning, then, that you are looking for the end? You see, the end will be where the beginning is.

Congratulations to the one who stands at the beginning: that one will know the end and will not taste death." *Jesus' statement refers to a level 4-5 psychedelic experience, it also refers to coming back to spiritual consciousness, which is where we started and will ultimately end. Read the levels of psychedelic experience, specifically the part in the "level 5" that refers to the beginning and the end of time, and reliving their own birth. This is no coincidence! At the beginning and ending of "time" is spiritual consciousness.*

19. Jesus said, "Congratulations to the one who came into being before coming into being.

If you become my disciples and pay attention to my sayings, these stones will serve you.

There are five trees in Paradise for you; they do not change, summer or winter, and their leaves do not fall. Whoever knows them will not taste death."

This refers to the spiritual awakening (coming into being, before permanent death) that happens after eating the fruit of knowledge. The part about the five trees is a blatant reference to the five levels of the psychedelic experience and also the mystical path. The part about the leaves not falling is a reference to a mushroom being the tree of knowledge, and the person who knows this truth and uses it can awaken their eternal spirit and once that happens, you will no longer fear death.

20. The disciples said to Jesus, "Tell us what Heaven's kingdom is like."

He said to them, "It's like a mustard seed, the smallest of all seeds, but when it falls on prepared soil, it produces a large plant and becomes a shelter for birds of the sky."

This refers to heaven's kingdom being within each of us, as the smallest amount of spiritual energy required to function. "Manna" (the magic mushroom) is nourishment for that energy. Once we are prepared to accept it and consume enough of it, then we will spiritually grow into a shelter for other spirits (or God) to work through. Magic mushrooms nourish the "God" within each of us. God truly dwells within each of us all you have do is learn how to bring him out.

21. Mary said to Jesus, "What are your disciples like?"

He said, "They are like little children living in a field that is not theirs. When the owners of the field come, they will say, 'Give us back our field.' They take off their clothes in front of them in order to give it back to them, and they return their field to them.

This is referring to the Gnostic secret of "the world" created by the Demiurge, and spiritual beings (children) masquerading in this world to show other unconscious spirits the truth about the fruit of knowledge and guide them back to spiritual consciousness. Upon the "harvest" (rapture) these "undercover" spirits, will remove their physical forms (the "clothes" of the physical world) and leave the negative physical world of the Demiurge.

For this reason I say, if the owners of a house know that a thief is coming, they will be on guard before the thief arrives and will not let the thief break into their house (their domain) and steal their possessions.

This refers to the Demiurge and his minions trying to keep us imprisoned here in our spiritual unconscious state as their "possessions", as Adam and Eve were a possession of the Demiurge (Satan) Christ and his disciples being a "thief" to steal as many of us as they could back to spiritual consciousness. There is a "veil of forgetfulness" around the "world". It was created by the devil. It is there to prevent any who come into "the world" from remembering their mission to spread the truth about the keys of knowledge being "the keys" to returning to spiritual consciousness.

As for you, then, be on guard against the world. Prepare yourselves with great strength, so the robbers can't find a way to get to you, for the trouble you expect, will come."

This refers to remaining focused on the goal of teaching others about the true keys of knowledge. He says "be on guard against the world", meaning: don't let yourselves be distracted by physical desire. The devil will use your physical desire against you. Only by focusing on the spiritual path and completely ignoring the physical path can you eliminate the devil's power to affect you. The devil is strong. He even uses your love of family and friends against you.

Let there be among you a person who understands.

When the crop ripened, he came quickly carrying a sickle and harvested it. Anyone here with two good ears had better listen!"

This refers to "the rapture", in which fully grown spirits will be harvested from this "world", back to spiritual consciousness. Only once you begin to consume the "manna" (magic mushrooms) will your spirits "ripen" (grow) and your perception change to a spiritual consciousness. Only then you will be ready to be harvested.

22. Jesus saw some babies nursing. He said to his disciples, "These nursing babies are like those who enter the (Father's) kingdom."

They said to him, "Then shall we enter the (Father's) kingdom as babies?"

Jesus said to them, "When you make the two into one, and when you

make the inner like the outer and the outer like the inner, and the upper like the lower, and when you make male and female into a single one, so that the male will not be male nor the female be female, when you make eyes in place of an eye, a hand in place of a hand, a foot in place of a foot, an image in place of an image, then you will enter [the kingdom]."

This refers to the separation of the two consciousnesses, one being in heaven and one being here, once you become spiritually conscious here, you will realize we are all equal, the differences between male and female are only physical differences, in God's eyes there are no differences between either, angels after all are unisex! Once you become spiritually whole (alive), and surrender your physical self (ego) to God's will, then you will be eligible to enter heaven. At that point it will be like being spiritually born, as a spiritual baby. Once you understand that when you are born into the physical world, there is only the smallest amount of spiritual energy (God) within you (the metaphor being, a baby is the smallest form of person who's entire goal is to grow), your entire goal should be to grow spiritually. Grow the "God" within you by consuming the "Manna" (magic mushrooms).

23. Jesus said, "I shall choose you, one from a thousand and two from ten thousand, and they will stand as a single one."

This refers to being chosen as "The Christ", the rare person who is willing to give up their physical life to become purely spiritual. The strength of will to experience "death" to bring forth the "God" within is very rare. This is the threshold you must pass to attain a "level 5" psychedelic experience. But remember once you have overcome the fear of "Death", you will not "taste" it.

24. His disciples said, "Show us the place where you are, for we must seek it."

He said to them, "Anyone here with two ears had better listen! There is light within a person of light, and it shines on the whole world. If it does not shine, it is dark."

This refers to someone who has been "chosen" to become "the one", should they not use their gift of knowledge to save the world (by helping everyone understand) then they are basically denying helping God. Personally, I would never knowingly deny him! Jesus used the fruit of knowledge to become spiritually awakened, and therefore discovered the "light" within himself. The light of God that shone through him upon the

"World" by teaching all who would listen of God's intention for us all to use the fruit of knowledge to come back to spiritual consciousness.

25. Jesus said, "Love your friends like you love your own soul, protect them like the pupil of your eye".

This refers to trying to keep your friends on the spiritual path. Free them as you freed yourself, by teaching them how to use the fruit of knowledge (magic mushrooms) to make themselves strong against the "world". Prevent the negativity and distractions of the "world" from affecting them and pulling them down the physical path, through anger, lust, greed, etc.

26. Jesus said, "You see the sliver in your friend's eye, but you don't see the timber in your own eye. When you take the timber out of your own eye, then you will see well enough to remove the sliver from your friend's eye."

This refers to how it is easy to see what others are doing wrong, but one rarely thinks about what they are doing wrong, once you master your own behavior, only then will you be ready to help your friend. Magic mushrooms force you to take a long hard look at yourself and this is what terrifies most people. When confronted by your true self what will you do? Will you let go of the physical you and embrace the spiritual you? Only once you learn to do that, will you be able to help anyone else do it.

27. "If you do not fast from the world, you will not find the (Father's) kingdom. If you do not observe the Sabbath as a Sabbath, you will not see the Father".

This refers to denying (or limiting) worldly (physical) desires, in order to focus on the spiritual path which leads back to spiritual consciousness and heaven. The Sabbath is meant as a day of worship and rest, but I believe in worshiping every day, not just once a week. Eat a heavy dose (3.5 dried grams or above) on Saturday night at 10 pm, then you will understand what it means to observe the Sabbath. Once you learn to use the "manna" to connect your spirit to God, the sheer overwhelmingness of the experience is so powerful and exhausting that it requires a full day of rest and reflection to comprehend even a little bit of it.

28. Jesus said, "I took my stand in the midst of the world, and in flesh I appeared to them. I found them all drunk, and I did not find any of them thirsty. My soul ached for the children of humanity, because they

are blind in their hearts and do not see, for they came into the world empty, and they also seek to depart from the world empty.

This refers to how he became spiritually awakened in "the world" and began to see how everyone is so full of teachings of people who seek to mislead them, and about how they are unwilling to even consider that they have been deceived. He preached the truth and they refused to listen. He was sad for the children because they came into the world without any true spiritual knowledge, and because of their deceived parents not teaching them the true spiritual lessons that they need to know, simply because they don't know what to teach, their children will only be taught the physical path without ever striving for spiritual knowledge. He used the "manna" to bring forth God within him (in flesh I appeared to them). He found "the world" full of people who had been deceived about the true purpose of the fruit of knowledge. The "truth", being the way to regain our connection to God through the use of the mushroom. They seek to depart the world empty because they refuse to open their mind to the truth about the fruit of knowledge because they refuse to see they've been deceived into thinking it's "forbidden".

29. Jesus said, "If the flesh came into being because of spirit, that is a marvel, but if spirit came into being because of the body, that is a marvel of marvels.

Yet I marvel at how this great wealth has come to dwell in this poverty."

This refers to empowering your spirit by weakening your body (fasting before the eating of Manna). Also how great spiritual wealth (knowledge) can be found by even those of poverty (magic mushrooms can be found for free in the wilderness [pasture]). He himself was not financially wealthy but spiritually, he was wealthier than all. You don't need to be financially wealthy to attain spiritual knowledge; in fact it is more difficult to do when you are financially wealthy. When you are "comfortable", you aren't likely to be so willing to give up that comfort. When you use the magic mushrooms to grow your spirit, you are in actuality "coming into being because of the body".

30. Jesus said, "Where there are three deities, they are divine. Where there are two or one, I am with that one."

This refers to being in the "kingdom", the father (God), the son (the humble servant), and the holy spirit (the "conscious" relationship between the father and the son), he also refers to how his eternal spirit will try and guide all who truly seek the truth". When you eat magic mushrooms, the psychedelic experience that happens has become known as a "trip". The definition of a trip is to go somewhere. When you eat magic mushrooms you take a spiritual trip back to the kingdom of God which is temporarily regaining spiritual consciousness. When you eat magic mushrooms you enter "the bridal suite" with God (when there are two or one). You will probably not understand this until you have your own psychedelic mushroom experience.

31. Jesus said, "No prophet is welcome on his own turf; doctors don't cure those who know them."

This refers to how one who becomes "the Christ", a prophet (a "spiritually awakened" messenger of God) through the use of the magic mushroom. He (or she) will not be able to convince those he knew before his spiritual awakening, because they will not be able to see past his previous faults to fully trust in him.

32. Jesus said, "A city built on a high hill and fortified cannot fall, nor can it be hidden".

This refers to one who strives for and attains spiritual perfection, cannot be defeated, and through the work of teaching others will become well known. Once you use the magic mushroom to defeat the negativity in your heart and unlock your spiritual self, it will be easy for others to see. The simplicity of spiritual truth that you speak of after you are spiritually awakened cannot be made complicated by organized religion's (the Pharisees) deceptions.

33. Jesus said, "What you will hear in your ear, in the other ear, proclaim from your rooftops.

He's referring to your spiritual ear, in which you receive spiritual guidance, that's what you should tell others, the simplicity of spiritual truth which you receive during the psychedelic mushroom experience. Once you feel the truth, you should show as many people as you can how to also find the truth for themselves. You should not reinforce the deceptions heard by the physical ear from the mouths of the Pharisees (organized religion).

After all, no one lights a lamp and puts it under a basket, nor does one put it in a hidden place. Rather, one puts it on a lampstand so that all who come and go will see its light."

This refers to what happens when one catches a glimpse of the spirit world during the psychedelic mushroom experience and becomes spiritually awakened, realizing they have found the truth; they seek to tell all who will listen. Once you are "enlightened" (lights a lamp) by the spiritual knowledge attained via the keys of knowledge, tell the world (so all who come and go will see).

34. Jesus said, "If a blind person leads a blind person, both of them will fall into a hole."

This refers to how confused unconscious spiritual priests in the luxurious church, guide other unconscious followers into confusion, possibly unknowingly, by denying the truth about the "Fruit of knowledge". They cannot teach the truth until they know it fully. The blind leading the blind, sadly that is the "world" (led by organized religion) as most know it.

35. Jesus said, "One can't enter a strong person's house and take it by force without tying his hands. Then one can loot his house."*This refers to how a prophet comes into "the world". By eating the "manna" one can become an awakened spirit undercover in physical form, who has learned the ways of the physical world so he can effectively navigate his way through it to reach trapped unconscious spirits in order to free them" [loot the demiurge's house]) By exposing the temptations (physical desires are simply the spiritual path's distractions) as they are, the spiritual one effectively prevents those temptations from having power (tying his hands).*

36. Jesus said, "Do not fret, from morning to evening and from evening to morning, [about your food—what you're going to eat, or about your clothing-] what you are going to wear. [You're much better than the lilies, which neither card nor spin.

As for you, when you have no garment, what will you put on? Who might add to your stature? That very one will give you your garment.]"

This refers to humility, eating and clothing are purely physical desires, a humble spirit thinks very little for food or clothing, he only eats what is required, not excess, and only covers his physical form not to offend or cause physical desire or distraction in others, not because they are ashamed. He speaks of the cloak of spirituality achieved through the use of manna (magic mushrooms), which makes you care very little about your physical appearance. In your spiritual form, which you will become aware of during the level 5 psychedelic experience, you will no longer feel the need for clothes, or the need to consume in order to live.

37. His disciples said, "When will you appear to us, and when will we see you?"

Jesus said, "When you strip without being ashamed, and you take your clothes and put them under your feet like little children and trample them, then [you] will see the son of the living one and you will not be afraid."*This refers to the understanding that our clothes are our bodies for our soul, once we take off our physical form, and return to spiritual consciousness, and we will no longer be afraid of death, because it was as simple as waking up. The psychedelic mushroom experience teaches you to take off your physical self, to cast it away willingly in order to return to spiritual consciousness. Once you have become comfortable with that transition from physical consciousness to spiritual consciousness (where God lives) you will understand death and not fear it.*

38. Jesus said, "Often you have desired to hear these sayings that I am speaking to you, and you have no one else from whom to hear them. There will be days when you will seek me and you will not find me". *This refers to how addictive the truth is. He was foretelling how the truth about what he was teaching (about the fruit of knowledge) would eventually be covered up by the church (by deeming them forbidden). He also foretold about how the church would tell lies "in Jesus' name" to lure people in, only to confuse them with more deception. Those who go to a building they call "church", look for God, because greedy people mislead them and tell them they can find God there, but they are looking in the wrong place. When you eat magic mushrooms and block out all physical distraction, you can find God by looking within, which magic mushrooms help you do. Eating magic mushrooms is going to church to me.*

39. Jesus said, "The Pharisees and the scholars have taken the keys of knowledge and have hidden them. They have not entered nor have they allowed those who want to enter to do so.

This is a blatant referral to the cover up of the fruit of knowledge, by changing the name to "forbidden fruit", and changing the image to an apple instead of a magic mushroom, they have effectively hidden the keys to the gates of heaven, and spiritual consciousness. (They have not entered the bridal suite with God) The keys to knowing yourself and finding heaven.

As for you, be as sly as snakes and as simple as doves."

Be sly by seeing through their deception about the fruit of knowledge and simplify your life by letting go of the physical distractions and focusing on the spiritual path. Physical entanglements only complicate our lives. Doves don't own anything. The more things you own, the more complicated your life becomes and the harder it is to focus on the spiritual path of simplicity.

40. Jesus said, "A grapevine has been planted apart from the Father. Since it is not strong, it will be pulled up by its root and will perish."

This refers to this "World". It has been placed apart from the Father (outside of heaven), it is corrupted and once we have all returned to spiritual consciousness, God will end this world along with the corruptions in it. During the psychedelic mushroom experience, one begins to understand how we are "apart" from the father.

41. Jesus said, "Whoever has something in hand will be given more, and whoever has nothing will be deprived of even the little they have."

This refers to how ownership of physical things creates an insatiable desire to own more things, whereas those who have nothing physical, will not be upset when nothing is deprived from them. The only thing they have is their physical life, if they freely give that up, then they will be rewarded with spiritual life. This is one of the things you will begin to understand during the psychedelic mushroom experience. This is why Jesus favored the poor. He knew it would be easier for them to give up their physical life. The magic mushroom teaches us how to let go. In the end of your physical life (the parole hearing) which comes for all of us, if you are "attached" to your physical things, you may not be able to "let go" of the physical world and will therefore be returned back to the physical world (will be given more). If you do not have any attachments to "the world" and no longer desire to be a part of it, you will be set free (welcomed back to spiritual consciousness, heaven).

42. Jesus said, "Be passersby."

This refers to what we all need to do in this temporal world. Come through this world temporarily without getting stuck on our journey back to spiritual consciousness [heaven]. Do not become so comfortable here that when it comes time to go, you are unwilling to leave. Our entire physical lives are simply a "road trip" down the road of life towards the final destination of heaven (spiritual consciousness). It's okay to enjoy the journey, just don't get so caught up trying to enjoy yourself that you don't make it to where you wanted to go before your car (your body) breaks down and you end up having to do it all over again (rebirth). This is what the magic mushroom does. It temporarily shows us our destination in order to help us not get side-tracked by physical distractions (the devil).

43. His disciples said to him, "Who are you to say these things to us?"

"You don't understand who I am from what I say to you.

Rather, you have become like the Judeans, for they love the tree but hate its fruit, or they love the fruit but hate the tree."

This refers to his disciples who knew him before he had his own spiritual experience via the magic mushroom and became "the Christ". Questioning him and dismissing his teachings because they didn't believe he was a prophet of God, simply because they knew him as a physical person, a peer. They loved him as a friend but hated his new found spirituality because that way of thinking wasn't the way his friends thought. Or they loved his words but didn't want to lose their physical friend which they saw as inevitable.

44. Jesus said, "Whoever blasphemes against the Father will be forgiven, and whoever blasphemes against the son will be forgiven, but whoever blasphemes against the Holy Spirit will not be forgiven, either on earth or in heaven."

This refers to never talking negatively about an individuals' intimate relationship with God (the Holy Spirit), to do so inspires others to do the same, which is doing the devils work. You can say whatever you like about me, your view of me is unimportant to me, but dare not talk negatively about my love for God and my effort to fulfill his plan to wake everyone up.

45. Jesus said, "Grapes are not harvested from thorn trees, nor are figs gathered from thistles, for they yield no fruit.

Good persons produce good from what they've stored up; bad persons produce evil from the wickedness they've stored up in their hearts, and say evil things. For from the overflow of the heart they produce evil." *This refers to why organized religion produces no spiritual simplicity (they yield no fruit). If they make it easy to understand, and teach people to find God through using the magic mushroom, people will* *no longer go to them to receive guidance and they will lose their weekly contributions. This also refers to how a person's mindset is contagious. A good and happy person fosters happiness and trust in others, and an angry person fosters anger, hostility, and distrust in others, even if that's not what they desire. Once you have your own psychedelic mushroom experience and your spiritual self begins to outgrow and overpower your physical self, everyone around you will begin to sense the goodness and spirituality emanating from you and it will cause them to also become spiritually stronger even though they might not realize it.*

46. Jesus said, "From Adam to John the Baptist, among those born of women, no one is so much greater than John the Baptist that his eyes should not be averted.

But I have said that whoever among you becomes a child will recognize the (Father's) kingdom and will become greater than John."

This refers to how we are all in this "world". And thus, being born of woman, we should never take our eyes off of the spiritual path and become distracted by, attracted to, or emotionally attached to the physical world or anything or anyone in it. He also refers to the fact that we are all capable of becoming a conscious child of God, because we are already God's children simply unconscious. We just don't realize that we are all children of God because of the "veil of forgetfulness" has removed our spiritual memory. This is what the magic mushroom reminds us of; that we are children of God (becomes a child).

47. Jesus said, "A person cannot mount two horses or bend two bows.

Referring to the two paths, or two consciousnesses, you must choose one. This is the lesson that magic mushrooms teach. They show you the difference of the two paths so that it is easier to concentrate on the right path. The physical path= Evil, darkness, confusion, death/ The spiritual path=Good, light, simplicity, life

And a slave cannot serve two masters, otherwise that slave will honor the one and offend the other.

Referring to full commitment to one path, again you must choose, physical path, "sins"= demiurge (satan)/ spiritual path, "virtues"= heaven (God). A better understanding is that once you come to understand that being physically conscious on earth is being in hell because we are distant from God while spiritually unconscious, to be in heaven is to be spiritually conscious, you will understand that you cannot be spiritually conscious and still have physical desires.

Nobody drinks aged wine and immediately wants to drink young wine.

Referring to how once you get a taste of the simpler spiritual path, after eating the "forbidden fruit" you will no longer desire the complicated physical path. Once you truly understand the difference between the two paths, it will be difficult for you to enjoy the physical path as you once did.

Young wine is not poured into old wineskins, or they might break, and aged wine is not poured into a new wineskin, or it might spoil.

This refers to why a spirit is reborn into this world without any spiritual knowledge. You must forget everything (churches deceptions) in order to learn everything (spiritual truth). You can't teach an old dog, new tricks.

An old patch is not sewn onto a new garment, since it would create a tear."

This refers to the age of innocence, and how young children are not capable of learning true spirituality except by parable [fairytales]) One must experience the physical world in order to understand the lesson that is to be physically "alive". The goal of living a physical life is to learn the lesson that physical desire only leads to unhappiness. Children are generally happy. Allow them to be that way through the age of innocence, so that they too can learn the lesson. As they mature, help them learn to let go of their physical desires so they can find spiritual happiness.

48. Jesus said, "If two make peace with each other in a single house, they will say to the mountain, 'Move from here!' and it will move."

This refers to one who unifies body and spirit, (By passing the test of the "level 5" psychedelic experience, overcoming the fear of death) and how every challenge they face after that will seem easy. Once you face "death", the challenges of the physical world take on a whole different perspective.

49. Jesus said, "Congratulations to those who are alone and chosen, for you will find the kingdom. For you have come from it, and you will return there again."

This refers to how we are all alone in this world, even if we have physical family and friends, we are still spiritually individual [alone], once you become spiritually awakened (by having a level 4-5 psychedelic mushroom experience) and are given (and choose to accept) spiritual guidance [chosen], you will understand the beginning (come from) and the end (will return). You will understand that you are here for a purpose and understand what that purpose is (to guide others back to spiritual consciousness). The ties that we form to our "loved" friends and family are nothing more than bindings to make it harder for us to leave.

50. Jesus said, "If they say to you, 'where have you come from?' say to them, 'We have come from the light, from the place where the light came into being by itself, established [itself], and appeared in their image.'

If they say to you, 'Is it you?' say, 'We are its children, and we are the chosen of the living Father.'

If they ask you, 'What is the evidence of your Father in you?' say to them, 'It is motion and rest.'"

(This refers to our spiritual energy. Our spiritual selves are children of God, and our spiritual energy (consciousness although unconscious) is what makes our bodies move (motion and rest). It is also our Father who will eventually call us home spiritually. [Physical death, a.k.a. "rest"]) By eating the fruit of knowledge and accepting what you learn from it, you will understand what it means to "come from the light".

51. His disciples said to him, "When will the rest for the dead take place, and when will the new world come?"

He said to them, "What you are looking forward to, has come, but you don't know it."

This refers to the judgment, where you will be held accountable for everything from your entire life. Reviewing everything from physical birth till physical death, every second, that would be like living. We are all already dead right now, this very moment (spiritually unconscious), and simply watching our lives play back in our judgment, without even realizing it. Death is the loss of conscious thought. We all spiritually "died" (lost spiritual consciousness) when we were physically "born". In actuality we simply "fell" unconscious due to a selfish poisoning, and we will only regain spiritual consciousness, once we use the spiritual cure, "manna", to give ourselves selflessly back to God.

52. His disciples said to him, "Twenty-four prophets have spoken in Israel, and they all spoke of you."

He said to them, "You have disregarded the living one who is in your presence, and have spoken of the dead."

This refers to how his disciples mentioned other physical people (the spiritually dead) in "The world" who have spoken of the "messiah", instead of listening to his teachings. He had already used the keys of knowledge (psychedelic mushrooms) to attain spiritual consciousness.

53. His disciples said to him, "Is circumcision useful or not?"

He said to them, "If it were useful, their father would produce children already circumcised from their mother. Rather, the true circumcision in spirit has become profitable in every respect."

This refers to how we have all been made as we should be; we already have everything we truly need. We all have an opportunity to regain our spiritual consciousness. Cutting back spiritual excess (confusion) leads to spiritual simplicity (happiness). Referencing the male penis in its uncircumcised form, it looks surprisingly similar to a beginning psilocybin mushroom. As the penis becomes erect, the head emerges, and the skin pulls and folds back resembling a maturing mushroom.

54. Jesus said, "Congratulations to the poor, for you belong to Heaven's kingdom."

This refers to the sin of greed, and how monetary wealth is coveted by physical people. The more you suffer in this world, the easier it will be to leave it when the time comes; poor people aren't comfortable enough in this world to want to stay. When your "physical" life is over, will you be ready for it to end, or will you fight the end? You will understand this if you eat magic mushrooms.

55. Jesus said, "Whoever does not hate father and mother cannot be my disciple, and whoever does not hate brothers and sisters, and carry the cross as I do, will not be worthy of me."

This refers to how one who is "chosen", must turn away from their temporary physical family, and also be willing to give up their temporary physical life in order to rejoin their eternal spiritual family. During the "test" which you take when you eat psilocybin mushrooms, you will be faced with the loss of everything you love in "the world", including your parents, children, friends, and even your own physical "life". Fear of loss will prevent you from passing your test, transcending and becoming one with the Holy Spirit (spiritually conscious). Only once you are ready to let everything go will you ascend. This is what magic mushrooms teach.

56. Jesus said, "Whoever has come to know the world has discovered a carcass, and whoever has discovered a carcass, of that person the world is not worthy."

This refers to someone who has had a level 5 psychedelic mushroom experience, which is like a near death experience, only temporary. This is what the fruit of knowledge does. It prepares you for the end of your physical life (transcendence). It shows you that you are already dead (spiritually unconscious), and what you know as your "life" is in actuality your "judgment". The selfish physical people of "the world", are not worthy of one who stays in "the world" (the spiritually unconscious state), with full knowledge of their own unconscious spiritual condition. Whoever has come to understand this knows how to return to heaven (spiritual consciousness), but remains in the unconscious state in order to guide others, even though they may be ungrateful. "The world" is not worthy of the one who is worthy of going to heaven (ready to go), but stays in hell for the sake of others.

57. Jesus said, "The Father's kingdom is like a person who has [good] seed. His enemy came during the night and sowed weeds among the good seed. The person did not let the workers pull up the weeds, but said to them, 'No, otherwise you might go to pull up the weeds and pull up the wheat along with them.' For on the day of the harvest the weeds will be conspicuous, and will be pulled up and burned."

This refers to the beginning of this world, how it was a nursery which was poisoned by selfishness and evil and how God told his angels not to remove anyone prematurely because they all have an equal chance to do good, and return to him and spiritual consciousness through the use of free will and the "manna". The "harvest" refers to the final judgment and "rapture" in which our spirits are "harvested" from our bodies. Once you have a "level 5" psychedelic experience and understand "the beginning and the end", you will understand this, for the psilocybin mushroom truly is "the fruit of knowledge". If you have not used the psilocybin mushroom to become one with God, at the end of your physical life it will be easy to tell.

58. Jesus said, "Congratulations to the person who has toiled and has found life."

This saying refers to the test of the psychedelic experience and how you must overcome barriers within your own mind (toiled) (overcoming your fear of death) in order to discover your true eternal spiritual self (consciousness/ life). It also refers to how we can live an entire temporary physical life without ever realizing the temporal nature of that physical life, instead of realizing that we are eternal spirits which will exist after this temporary place (in everlasting life), and not to focus on the physical while forsaking the spiritual. One who has worked to see through the deceptions to find the spiritual truth. Do not focus on the temporary. Understand that your physical life and everything in it, is only temporary. Instead use the "manna" to focus on your eternal spiritual life and allow all the temporary things to fade away.

59. Jesus said, "Look to the living one as long as you live, otherwise you might die and then try to see the living one, and you will be unable to see."

This refers to what the psychedelic experience does for you. It is spiritual training, it allows you to temporarily experience "death" (transcendence) in order to help you realize the spirit world is real, so that when permanent physical death takes you to the spirit world, you know what to expect and you become fully spiritually conscious. If you understand death as simply waking up, you will not fear it. By fearing passage to the spirit world, you effectively prevent yourself from going to heaven, simply because you don't understand it as it is, and it is in our nature to fear something we don't understand. That after all was one of the ways that Lucifer trapped us here in the first place, by making us fear our physical death. You can't see the top floor of the stairway to heaven from the first step. He's telling us to use the "manna" to find our spiritual path, and then continue using it to then stay focused on that path in order to overcome this physical prison. The simple truth is: Eating psilocybin mushrooms is going "to the church within" and looking to the living one. He's telling us to use magic mushrooms regularly in order to keep your bond to God and spiritual consciousness strong so that when your physical life ends, it is easier for you to let go of the physical world.

60. He saw a Samaritan carrying a lamb and going to Judea. He said to his disciples, "That person [carries] around the lamb." They said to him, "So that he may kill it and eat it." He said to them, "He will not eat

it while it is alive, but only after he has killed it and it has become a carcass."

They said, "Otherwise he can't do it."

He said to them, "So also with you, seek for yourselves a place for rest, or you might become a carcass and be eaten."

This refers to how this physical world and the Demiurge are consuming our spiritual energy in order to continue his spiritual life outside of heaven. Use magic mushrooms to find heaven (a place for rest) while you are "alive" so that your spiritual energy is not consumed by the devil (physical world).

61. Jesus said, "Two will recline on a couch; one will die, one will live."

Salome said, "Who are you mister? You have climbed onto my couch and eaten from my table as if you are from someone."

Jesus said to her, "I am the one who comes from what is whole. I was granted from the things of my Father."

"I am your disciple."

"For this reason I say, if one is whole, one will be filled with light, but if one is divided, one will be filled with darkness."

This refers again to the psychedelic mushroom experience. During a level 4-5 experience, spiritual/physical separation occurs, therefore physical movement becomes difficult (reclining on a couch), at that level, spiritual understanding occurs and physical desires are lessened or removed completely. Therefore your spiritual self (consciousness, the part of God within you) will begin (become whole) and your physical self (your ego), (the part of the devil within you) will die (only the states of mind live and die). He also refers to how he completely went to the spirit world back to full spiritual consciousness (whole) and returned (was "granted" by consuming the fruit of knowledge- "the things of my Father"-God's mushroom) to help others. The psilocybin mushroom experience shows you what it is to be "whole" (completely in tune with your spiritual path. To be committed to God's will and plan 100%). If you still have physical desire (to be "divided", not committed 100%) it will be much easier for the devil to distract you with temporary physical things.

62. Jesus said, "I disclose my mysteries to those [who are worthy] of [my] mysteries.

This refers to why a physically dominated person has a hard time understanding the parables. His "mysteries" (teachings) are easy to understand for someone who has had a spiritual awakening (psychedelic experience). If you refuse to believe anything other than what the organized religions (Pharisees) teach, you will never find the "keys of knowledge" (manna) and become worthy to understand the spiritual truth that he taught.

63. Jesus said, "There was a rich person who had a great deal of money. He said, 'I shall invest my money so that I may sow, reap, plant, and fill my storehouses with produce, that I may lack nothing.' These were the things he was thinking in his heart, but that very night he died. Anyone here with two ears had better listen!"

This refers to a person who is only concerned with his temporary physical life, and when you physically die, you leave all of those temporary physical things behind, and begin a spiritual life. He began his spiritual life with nothing. Instead, we should focus on spiritual growth in this life, so we lack nothing when it comes time for our temporary physical lives to end and we begin our spiritual lives. You can never be sure when you will meet your physical end; you might as well get busy working on your spiritual beginning. The rich person devoted his entire physical life to the physical path, never bothering to pay any mind to the spiritual path which he should have been focusing on. Everything in the physical world is temporary. Do not focus your mind on your temporary physical path. Use the fruit of knowledge to awaken your unconscious spirit. Once you've awakened your spirit, continue using the "manna" to grow your spirit. Make your spiritual growth more important than your physical path and comfort so that when your physical end comes, your spirit lacks nothing (be prepared for transcendence).

64. Jesus said, "A person was receiving guests. When he had prepared the dinner, he sent his slave to invite the guests.

The slave went to the first and said to that one, 'My master invites you.' That one said, 'Some merchants owe me money; they are coming to me tonight. I have to go and give them instructions. Please excuse me from dinner.'

The slave went to another and said to that one, 'My master has invited you.' That one said to the slave, 'I have bought a house, and I have been called away for a day. I shall have no time.'

The slave went to another and said to that one, 'My master invites you.' That one said to the slave, 'My friend is to be married, and I am to arrange the banquet. I shall not be able to come. Please excuse me from dinner.'

The slave went to another and said to that one, 'My master invites you.' That one said to the slave, 'I have bought an estate, and I am going to collect the rent. I shall not be able to come. Please excuse me.'

The slave returned and said to his master, 'Those whom you invited to dinner have asked to be excused.' The master said to his slave, 'Go out on the streets and bring back whomever you find to have dinner.'

Buyers and merchants [will] not enter the places of my Father."

This is a simple parable. It refers to how God has invited us all to return to spiritual consciousness (heaven) through the consumption of a special spiritual food (psilocybin mushrooms), and due to most of us being consumed and distracted by physical desire (fear of death), (physically focused instead of spiritually focused, distracted by the devil) we choose not to go, even though we don't know what we're missing. Though those who are on the street (the poor, the humble, the non-distracted by desire to collect money or own things), would be sure to come to dinner. The spiritually hungry would gladly take an offer of spiritual fulfillment. Use the fruit of knowledge to understand the difference between the physical and spiritual paths. God will accept anyone who is able to overcome the poison of physical desire. This is the true goal of our life journey.

65. He said, "A person owned a vineyard and rented it to some farmers, so they could work it and he could collect its crop from them. He sent his slave so the farmers would give him the vineyard's crop. They grabbed him, beat him, and almost killed him, and the slave returned and told his master. His master said, 'Perhaps he didn't know them.' He sent another slave, and the farmers beat that one as well. Then the master sent his son and said, 'Perhaps they'll show my son some respect.' Because the farmers knew that he was the heir to the vineyard, they grabbed him and killed him. Anyone here with two good ears had better listen!"

(This refers to how this world was once a spiritual nursery where spirits were grown through the use of psilocybin mushrooms "manna", and then harvested to be in God's kingdom, but the devil stole the nursery and it's crops from God (by deeming God's mushroom "forbidden"), and everyone who has been sent to retrieve the crops (god's spiritual children) has been hurt or killed by the demiurges minions (the church) Everyone who has tried

to expose the truth that I'm telling you now has been deemed a "heretic" and been beaten or put to death, because "the church" hides the truth in order to make a profit and seek to prevent anyone from going to heaven.

66. Jesus said, "Show me the stone that the builders rejected: that is the keystone."

This refers to how his teachings (about the key to spiritual consciousness [his father's kingdom] being psilocybin mushrooms) were rejected by the organized religions of the time, and how they deemed the fruit of knowledge "Forbidden". The builders of modern society (sadly) are "the church" (organized religion, a.k.a. the Pharisees). The stone they rejected is the fruit of knowledge (psilocybin mushrooms). Magic mushrooms are the keys to the gates of heaven.

67. Jesus said, "Those who know all, but are lacking in themselves, are utterly lacking."

This refers to people who are wise only in the ways of the physical world, and know very little or nothing at all about their true spiritual nature. Psilocybin mushrooms allow you to discover and grow your spiritual self through introspective meditation.

68. Jesus said, "Congratulations to you when you are hated and persecuted; and no place will be found, wherever you have been persecuted."

This refers to when you become spiritually enlightened through the true beauty that is the psychedelic mushroom experience. When you begin to guide others away from their organized religions who keep them confused, those organized religions will hate you and will no longer welcome you, because you will be taking away their weekly collections, and showing them as frauds, the same way that Jesus did. Once you show people the truth, it will be harder to deceive them.

69. Jesus said, "Congratulations to those who have been persecuted in their hearts: they are the ones who have truly come to know the Father."

This refers to the inner turmoil that happens along the mystic path as one progresses through the five levels of psychedelic mushroom experience and when you've had a level 5 psychedelic mushroom experience, you will understand the inner persecution that he's referring to, and you will know the Father.

Congratulations to those who go hungry, so the stomach of the one in want may be filled."

This refers to the mystic practice of weakening the physical self by fasting before consuming the fruit of knowledge in order to make it easier to achieve spiritual transcendence. The intentional weakening of your physical prison in order to gain spiritual fulfillment and freedom, is where "fasting" in religion comes from. It's not for financial gain! To think about it financially is to be physically focused. The "stomach of the one in want" is the stomach of your spiritual self. To fill a "stomach" you must eat something. To fill a "spiritual stomach" you must eat a spiritual food. Magic mushrooms contain very little physical nutritional value, but their spiritual value is incredible. You must try them to understand.

70. Jesus said, "If you bring forth what is within you, what you have will save you. If you do not have that within you, what you do not have within [will] kill you."

This refers to faith and trust in God. While in the midst of a level 4-5 psychedelic mushroom experience, you temporarily experience spiritual/physical separation, this is an experience that many sadly only experience upon physical death, and therefore are unprepared for it. The physical mind is incapable of comprehending the difference between temporary and permanent spiritual/physical separation, so at this level a "bad trip" (the fear of death) is experienced due to the fear that accompanies that unknown experience. Although, if you have faith and trust in God, and believe completely, 100%, that he only wants what is best for you, and surrender yourself completely to him, (learn to completely let go) you will be "saved" on many levels. Focus on trying to understand what God wants from you (focus on God's love). Do not be distracted by "self" preservation (fear of death is a bad trip).

71. Jesus said, "I will destroy [this] house, and no one will be able to build it [...].

This refers to the Gnostic belief that this "world" was created (or at least corrupted) by the Demiurge, and at this point it is considered a loss by our spiritual Father. He hasn't destroyed it yet due to the fact that the Devil still holds us hostage (in our spiritually unconscious state), inside of it and he loves us so greatly. Once we all use the fruit of knowledge to return to spiritual consciousness, the Demiurge will run out of food and his illusion will fail and he will die. All the negativity of the world will disappear.

72. A [person said] to him, "Tell my brothers to divide my father's possessions with me."

He said to the person, "Mister, who made me a divider?"

He turned to his disciples and said to them, "I'm not a divider, am I?"

This refers to the difference between a physical father and our spiritual father. To care about a physical father's possessions is the physical (evil) path. Our spiritual Father's possession is simply love, and God's love cannot be divided. It can be obtained wholly simply by seeking it out and accepting it. Jesus did not deal out God's love. He showed others how to find it for themselves, by consuming the fruit of knowledge, and helping them experience their own, "level 5" psychedelic mushroom experience.

73. Jesus said, "The crop is huge but the workers are few, so beg the harvest boss to dispatch workers to the fields."

This is referring to the need for more enlightened people to guide "the confused" back to spiritual consciousness. It also refers to Jesus' understanding that he could not complete his goal of awakening everyone in the world on his own, and asking for help from his apostles (more enlightened disciples). He encouraged others to save themselves by using the keys of knowledge and then work to save others through an effort to spread the truth that the Pharisees and Catholic Church had tried to hide. Once you have used the psilocybin mushrooms (the antidote for our spiritual unconsciousness) to awaken yourself, become a "worker" and help others to awaken themselves by showing them the power of God's mushroom. As long as there is an unconscious person in the physical world, the devil will remain. It is up to us to defeat him, and we do that by revealing this truth.

74. He said, "Lord, there are many around the drinking trough, but there is nothing in the well."

This simply refers to the total lack of spiritual truth in religion and "the world" in general. He was referring to the amount of people in the world who truly want to believe, but just don't know what to believe and feel spiritually as if they are being mislead, because the church preaches deception (by deeming the fruit of knowledge "forbidden") instead of spiritual truth. Due to the cover up of the fruit of knowledge, the well of truth and spiritual knowledge has run dry.

75. Jesus said, "There are many standing at the door, but those

who are alone will enter the bridal suite."

This refers to the many people in the "world" who seek spiritual enlightenment. Due to being confused by their blindly following of people who are incapable of leading them, they don't know that they have two selves, the physical and spiritual. Once they use the fruit of knowledge (magic mushrooms) to understand that simple truth and become able to let go of their physical self and become spiritually alone, can they attain spiritual completeness (Have their own "level 5 psychedelic mushroom experience and enter the bridal suite with God. Become one with God).

76. Jesus said, "The Father's Kingdom is like a merchant who had a supply of merchandise and found a pearl. That merchant was prudent; he sold the merchandise and bought the single pearl for himself.

So also with you, seek his treasure that is unfailing, that is enduring, where no moth comes to eat and no worm destroys."

This refers to the treasure of spiritual enlightenment (the knowledge learned by using the "fruit of knowledge" and having a "level 5" experience) which is permanent, and removal of temporary physical treasures (distractions), because nothing physical is permanent. Spiritual knowledge is the only treasure that is unfailing. This is what the psilocybin mushroom experience gives us, spiritual knowledge and an intimate experience of God's love.

77. Jesus said, "I am the light that is over all things. I am all; from me all came forth, and to me all attained.

Split a piece of wood; I am there.

Lift up the stone, and you will find me there."

This refers to the feeling of oneness with everything in the universe that is achieved with a level 4-5 psychedelic mushroom experience.

78. Jesus said, "Why have you come out to the countryside? To see a reed shaken by the wind? And to see a person dressed in soft clothes, [like your] rulers and your powerful ones? They are dressed in soft clothes, and they cannot understand truth."

This refers to people who look to Jesus as a physical leader instead of seeing him as he truly was, a spiritual guide. It also refers to physical rulers and powerful (comfortable) physical people; not understanding spiritual truth because it is exactly opposite to physical belief. Spiritual truth will make a physical person uncomfortable. They do not try to, and therefore cannot, understand spiritual truth because they do not wish to give up their comfort (dressed in soft clothes).

79. A woman in the crowd said to him, "Lucky are the womb that bore you and the breasts that fed you."

He said to [her], "Lucky are those who have heard the word of the Father and have truly kept it. For there will be days when you will say, 'Lucky are the womb that has not conceived and the breasts that have not given milk.'"

This refers to the understanding that we are all born into hell (A spiritual unconscious state), and how our physical ties (the love of our physical children and family) keep us here, because one that has no children or family, has nothing to stay for, and in that respect, it will be easier for them to leave this physical consciousness behind and attain spiritual consciousness. It is more difficult for one who has children to have the "level 5" psychedelic experience and master transcendence because the devil uses your love for them against you in order to prevent you from leaving your physical consciousness to achieve spiritual consciousness and oneness with God. When you've had a "level 5" psychedelic mushroom experience, and have come to understand God's plan (heard the word of the father), and have worked towards helping him fulfill his goal of awakening his unconscious children (have truly kept it), you have basically mastered the ability to have complete unwavering focus on your spiritual path and growth.

80. Jesus said, "Whoever has come to know the world has discovered the body, and whoever has discovered the body, of that one the world is not worthy."

This refers to the understanding of the difference between the physical and spiritual selves. "Out-of-body" experiences are common when you eat psilocybin mushrooms and go above the "level 3" psychedelic experience. Once you understand (come to know) "the world" as an illusion of your unconscious spiritual mind, and see your body as a mere suit, designed to allow your spiritual consciousness to navigate the illusionary physical world, the world of unconscious people will not be worthy of you, although that doesn't mean you don't still have a job to do. Now get to work at the task of waking everyone else up by spreading this truth!

81. Jesus said, "Let one who has become wealthy reign, and let one

who has power renounce it".

This refers to spiritual wealth (knowledge), and giving up control (power). What we need in this world is a humble spiritual leader, capable of helping even the feeblest of minds, find their own spiritual truth, instead of some power hungry physical leader only concerned with their own superiority and controlling how others think and act (power). When you become spiritually "awakened" through the use of psilocybin mushrooms and then begin guiding others, you will gain popularity beyond that of any "elected" official. Don't become so attached to the popularity that you become comfortable and unable to walk away from it. (renounce it)

82. Jesus said, "Whoever is near me is near the fire, and whoever is far from me is far from the (Father's) Kingdom."

This refers to spiritual consciousness. Through the 5 levels of psychedelic mushroom experience, one can come closer and closer to spiritual consciousness, and with that knowledge, can begin to understand ascension to heaven, (complete spiritual consciousness). "Near the fire" referring to the warmth of God's love, and "Far from the Kingdom", referring to how in an unconscious state, a person is distant to the conscious world, (a.k.a. dead to the world). We are all distant from God, because to him, we are all unconscious. He created the "manna" to show us this very fact so we could wake up, because he misses us.

83. Jesus said, "Images are visible to people, but the light within them is hidden in the image of the Father's light. He will be disclosed, but his image is hidden by his light."

This refers to the virtual reality of this world. As long as we are focused completely on our perceived physical environments, it will be difficult to see the spiritual path that had been right in front of us the entire time. We will only be able to see things completely clearly upon complete spiritual consciousness (physical death, either temporarily through the psilocybin mushroom experience or permanent). The physical world's (the devils) distractions, tend (are designed) to take our focus away from spiritual truth. During the psychedelic mushroom experience, auras can be seen emanating from people and objects (what is hidden will be revealed).

84. Jesus said, "When you see your likeness, you are happy. But when you see your images that came into being before you and that neither die nor become visible, how much you will have to bear!"

This is a blatant reference to a level 4-5 psychedelic experience. Ignorance is bliss. As long as you are only aware of your physical existence (self) you will not see anything wrong with it, and it is easy to enjoy. But once you have a level 4-5 experience and become "aware" of your "pre-mortal" existence, (spiritual self), and the evil, deceiving insatiable nature of your physical self, you will no longer be able to enjoy the physical activities which distracted us from seeking the spiritual path as you once did. Once you truly learn your lesson, you cannot un-learn it. It is a difficult task to explain this to a person who is physically consumed (spiritually unconscious), but try you must! Read the "Wikipedia" definition of the 5 levels of psychedelic experience, specifically the "level 5" section which tells of people feeling like they had existed for thousands of years as transparent entities or smoke. This is no coincidence!

85. Jesus said, "Adam came from great power and great wealth, but he was not worthy of you. For had he been worthy, [he would] not [have tasted] death."

This refers to Adam only eating of the "forbidden fruit" once, and after that deciding not to eat it again and return to full spiritual consciousness. Instead he chose to further follow his physical path, by pursuing Eve, and fathering physical children. Adam was one of the original "fallen" angels who fell in love with the physical path and Eve. By being distracted by physical desire, he helped the devil by fathering more unconscious children in his unconscious state.

86. Jesus said, "[Foxes have] their dens and birds have their nests, but human beings have no place to lay down and rest."

This refers to the understanding that we as humans (our spiritual selves) were never meant for this (physical) world. Every creature in this world has a purpose. They all have a part to play in the bigger picture, except us. Physical humans are consumers. We are consuming this planet instead of protecting it, just like the Demiurge consumes us. We are meant to use the manna (magic mushrooms) and transcend to spiritual consciousness. We have overstayed our time here.

87. Jesus said, "How miserable is the body that depends on a body, and how miserable is the soul that depends on these two."

This refers to being in this world as a spiritual person, with the understanding that in order to fulfill your purpose in this world (spiritually awakening others) you have to continue operating your physical body (vessel), even though you would rather not because you understand its evil nature and see it as a channel for evil through its own insatiable physical desires. Physically consumed people are also miserable even though they don't know it, again ignorance is bliss. Every day in the physical world is a battle against being distracted away from the spiritual path to fulfilling God's goal.

88. Jesus said, "The messengers and the prophets will come to you and give you what belongs to you. You, in turn, give them what you have, and say to yourselves, 'When will they come and take what belongs to them?"

This refers to spiritual consciousness. The true messengers and prophets will guide you back to spiritual consciousness, therefore giving you your true self and your own salvation through teaching you to use the psilocybin mushroom. In turn you should give them your unnecessary physical possessions and effort to help further their work (the work of helping others experience God's love through the use of the sacred mushroom). Once you become spiritually "awake", you will long for God's angels to come back and reclaim you (the end of your physical life) for it is your spiritual self who belongs to God and his angels (his angels being an extension of him and his kingdom).

89. Jesus said, "Why do you wash the outside of the cup? Don't you understand that the one who made the inside is also the one who made the outside?

This refers to spiritual cleansing. Many people focus on cleaning their physical selves (bodies), but their spiritual selves are filthy. Instead we should focus less on our physical selves and concentrate more on our spiritual selves. When you eat the psilocybin mushroom, your focus shifts inward and you begin to de-clutter your spirit.

90. Jesus said, "Come to me, for my yoke is comfortable and my lordship is gentle, and you will find rest for yourselves."

This refers to spiritual consciousness, "rest" meaning physical death. When you separate from your physical self, your spiritual self is released from the work of making your physical self function. (Released from work= rest) The will of God (to awaken his spiritual children) is a spiritually rewarding job and is not difficult for one with the Holy Spirit (a complete connection to God). This you will only understand once you have experienced a "level 5" psychedelic experience.

91. They said to him, "Tell us who you are so that we may believe in you."

He said to them, "You examine the face of heaven and earth, but you have not come to know the one who is in your presence, and you do not know how to examine the present moment."

This refers to their spiritually unconscious selves, that God is with them spiritually they just don't know it because they are spiritually unconscious. They don't realize the present moment is a moment of eternity (our entire physical lives go by in this mere moment of eternity) in which we are all judged (also known as life, yes, this is that moment). Eat the "manna" and you will understand. The judgment is nothing more than whether or not you are able to let go of physical desire or the desire to have a physical life. It is your choice that no one can make for you!

92. Jesus said, "Seek and you will find".

In the past however, I did not tell you the things about which you asked me then. Now I am willing to tell them, but you are not seeking them."

This refers to his physically concerned disciples, asking him to give them pure, spiritual truths, but due to their focus on their physical path, those truths were withheld from them because Jesus knew they wouldn't understand, and because they couldn't fully deny their physical path, they are still not seeking his spiritual wisdom. Seek the truth about the "forbidden fruit" for yourself and you will find it, by comparing the biblical descriptions of "manna" to the psilocybin mushroom. Consume the true "manna" and use the "keys of knowledge" to unlock your ability to understand the meanings of the Gospel of Thomas.

93. Don't give what is holy to dogs, for they might throw them upon the manure pile. Don't throw pearls [to] pigs, or they might [defile]... it [...]."

This refers to his teachings about the "keys of knowledge" being "pearls of wisdom" and the corruptions of the documentations of his sermons. His references to dogs and pigs, were meant to represent the luxurious Roman Catholic Church (the Pharisees), and other powerful organized religions who sought to undo (defile) his teaching of the use of the "forbidden" fruit of knowledge (pearl of spiritual knowledge) by deeming his teachings "heretical" and the fruit of knowledge "forbidden".

94. Jesus [said], "One who seeks will find, and for [one who knocks] it will be opened."

The "one who seeks" refers to a person who takes it upon themselves to find God and his Kingdom (salvation) through the use of God's sacred mushroom ("manna"), instead of relying on the deceptions of organized religion to save them, you "knock" when you eat psilocybin mushrooms and open the door of consciousness by having a "level 5" psychedelic experience.

95. [Jesus said], "If you have money, don't lend it at interest. Rather, give [it] to someone from whom you won't get it back."

This simply refers to not caring for physical wealth as much as the spiritual happiness of helping others. Do not value physical things (give them to someone whom you won't get them back). Value spiritual knowledge and the opportunity to help God fulfill his will above all physical things and share that with everyone you can. Happiness is in simplicity. The more things you own the more complicated your life becomes and the harder it is to be simply happy.

96. Jesus [said], "The Father's kingdom is like [a] woman. She took a little heaven, [hid] it in dough, and made it into large loaves of bread. Anyone here with two ears had better listen!"

This refers to how this world was designed as a spiritual nursery in which to grow spirits for our spiritual Father's kingdom. A little bit of spiritual energy grows in each of us (a little bit of heaven hidden in physical form) until it is ready to be removed. It could also be a reference to baking with "manna". Use "manna" (magic mushrooms) to grow your spirit so that you will be fully grown when it comes time to harvest you.

97. Jesus said, "The [Father's] kingdom is like a woman who was carrying a [jar] full of meal. While she was walking along [a] distant road, the handle of the jar broke and the meal spilled behind her along the road. She didn't know it; she hadn't noticed a problem. When she reached her house, she put the jar down and discovered that it was empty."

This refers to how things are. We do not know that there is a problem until it is too late. In other words, we go through our entire physical lives being drained of our spiritual energy, without knowing it, until we reach the end, only to realize that we no longer have any left and realize it's too late to get any of it back. The physical world drains our spiritual energy. By using the "manna" (magic psilocybin mushrooms) to learn how to detach ourselves from the physical world, we can notice "the problem" and stop the spiritual drainage, so that when we reach the end of the road of "life" we will not be "empty".

98. Jesus said, "The Father's Kingdom is like a person who wanted to kill someone powerful. While still at home he drew his sword and thrust it into the wall to find out whether his hand would go in. Then he killed the powerful one."

This refers to devaluing physical things in order to kill your insatiable physical desires, (the powerful one) Once you use the "manna", your spiritual self will "wake up" and you will understand physical things don't matter, and the physical temptations will lose their power over you. Magic psilocybin mushrooms can help your spiritual self overcome your physical desire (kill the powerful one).

99. The disciples said to him, "Your brothers and your mother are standing outside."

He said to them, "Those here who do what my Father wants are my brothers and my mother. They are the ones who will enter my Father's kingdom."

This refers to his mission and the Apostles mission of trying to guide others back to spiritual consciousness, (by teaching about the "keys of knowledge") because that is God's plan,(doing what his father wants) to wake up all of his unconscious spiritual children. He was referring to spiritual family which can be different than physical family. God wants us all to eat magic mushrooms and return to spiritual consciousness (heaven). God also wants us all to teach everyone who is unaware of the mushrooms power to use it to reunite with him.

100. They showed Jesus a gold coin and said to him, "The Roman emperor's people demand taxes from us."

He said to them, "Give the emperor what belongs to the emperor, give God what belongs to God, and give me what is mine."

This refers to how government (the devil's minions) made the money in order to enslave and distract people. It came from them and therefore it belongs to them, they just loan it to us (at interest, "taxes"). God gave us our soul, (spiritual energy) it came from him and therefore it belongs to him (he just loans it to us). Jesus gave spiritual truth, and all he wants is to help God by guiding others back to spiritual consciousness, completing his duty. To believe in his teachings (of the fruit of knowledge) and understand them and therefore returning to spiritual consciousness, through trust in God's plan through believing in his teachings, gives him honor. Jesus only wanted the satisfaction of successfully completing the task that god put before him, which was to guide all the people of the world back to spiritual consciousness by teaching them to use the mushroom. Don't work for money. Work to complete God's will. Work to spread the truth about the "forbidden" fruit.

101. "Whoever does not hate [father] and mother as I do cannot be my [disciple], and whoever does [not] love [father and] mother as I do cannot be my [disciple]. For my mother [...], but my true [mother] gave me life."

This refers to knowing the difference between physical father and mother, and spiritual Father and Mother. To understand that our physical parents unknowingly imprisoned us spiritually in an imperfect world run by the Demiurge will cause us to see them negatively [hate]. In turn, God is both our Spiritual Father and Mother in one, and it is from God that we have our spiritual energy and life; therefore we should love God with all our soul as Jesus did. Ultimate devotion to God, our spiritual father, is being willing to give up your physical life to return to him, as Jesus did! Magic mushrooms help you understand this.

102. Jesus said, "Damn the Pharisees! They are like a dog sleeping in the cattle manger: the dog neither eats nor [lets] the cattle eat."

This refers to how "organized" religious leaders don't follow their true spiritual path (by denying the truth about the "fruit of knowledge"), and in turn, force the confused followers of "their" religions to follow the physical path, even though they desire to follow their spiritual path. Because they do not strive for spiritual perfection through the use of the "keys of knowledge" (magic mushrooms), they do not allow or help others attain spiritual perfection. (by deeming them "forbidden" and disguising their true identity by changing it to an apple, they prevented their followers [the cattle] from eating) Instead of teaching people how to live "properly" religion should show people how to die "properly". This is the "knowledge" learned from the "fruit of knowledge", how to let go of the physical world to attain spiritual consciousness. Attaining spiritual consciousness (going to heaven) is a learned ability, which organized religion fails to teach.

103. Jesus said, "Congratulations to those who know where the rebels are going to attack. [They] can get going, collect their imperial resources, and be prepared before the rebels arrive."

This refers to the war in heaven, Armageddon, and "the rapture". To understand that this world is the battle ground where the battle is fought inside each and every one of us, (the battle between our physical and spiritual selves) enables us to win our own personal battles and be able to overcome any negative attack on our positive spirits. Luck favors the prepared. It is easier to fight a battle that you know is going on. This is what magic mushrooms do, they help you understand the internal struggle between your physical and spiritual selves so that you become immune to the effects of physical desire (how the rebels attack).

104. They said to Jesus, "Come, let us pray today, and let us fast."

Jesus said, "What sin have I committed, or how have I been undone? Rather, when the groom leaves the bridal suite, then let people fast and pray."

This refers to the intimate relationship between one who is totally committed to God and God (one with the Holy Spirit). He has no need to specifically pray, because his mind is constantly praying already (internally walking the spiritual path with God, being strong against physical desire). When a person gives into physical desire (the groom leaves the bridal suite), (sins) and forsakes their spiritual path (ignores their intimate relationship with God) only then do they need to refocus themselves on their spiritual path through prayer and physical self denial (fasting).

105. Jesus said, "Whoever knows the father and the mother will be called the child of a whore".

This reference relates to the ancient view of heresy. Due to Jesus' awakening and proclamation that he was a child of God, or a son of God, he was deemed a heretic. Jesus taught people to find God outside of the "church" which was also seen as "heresy". A "heretic" being viewed negatively, this is similar to the negative view of a physically fatherless child of a whore.

106. Jesus said, "When you make the two into one, you will become children of Adam, and when you say, 'Mountain, move from here!' it will move."

This refers to the spiritual awakening that happens upon a conscious level 5 psychedelic mushroom experience. Once you become fully spiritually conscious (and one with God) through the use of "Manna", no physical barrier will be able to stand before you. There will be no challenge in the physical world too difficult for you to overcome once you've used the magic mushroom to overcome your fear of death.

107. Jesus said, "The (Father's) Kingdom is like a shepherd who had a hundred sheep. One of them, the largest, went astray. He left the ninety-nine and looked for the one until he found it. After he had toiled, he said to the sheep, 'I love you more than the ninety-nine.'"

This refers to us. We (our spiritual selves) are God's sheep and he is our shepherd. The more committed we are to our spiritual path the larger our spiritual selves grow. Once we've committed ourselves fully to our spiritual path, our shepherd will work to keep us on that path instead of going astray down the physical path. Full commitment is what's required to attain the "level 5" psychedelic experience. Fear is the absence of love. God truly loves someone who is willing to die for him. This is what the "manna" does; it proves how far you are willing to go for God.

108. Jesus said, "Whoever drinks from my mouth will become like me; I myself shall become that person, and the hidden things will be revealed to him."

This refers to his teachings (of the keys of knowledge, "manna"). To accept his teaching and understand it (as unorthodox and different as it was), is symbolized by "drinking from his mouth". It refers to anyone (whoever) having the ability to become "the Christ", by using the "fruit of knowledge" (drink from my mouth) to come to understand "the world" as it truly is (the hidden truth will be revealed).

109. Jesus said,"The (Father's) kingdom is like a person who had a treasure hidden in his field but did not know it. And [when] he died he left it to his [son]. The son [did] not know about it either. He took over the field and sold it. The buyer went plowing, [discovered] the treasure, and began to lend money at interest to whomever he wished."

This refers to the understanding that the key to understanding our spiritual guidance (the antidote for our poison known as physical desire is the treasure) grows naturally all over the world (our field), but due to it being deemed "forbidden", and its image changed to an apple, it has been hidden from us. Centuries have gone by and generations have come and gone from the "field" without realizing its existence and value, but the spiritual truth is trying to come out and I (the buyer) have figured it out and wish to pass it to you. I will do my part for God.

110. Jesus said, "Let one who has found the world, and has become wealthy, renounce the world."

This refers to someone who has had a level 3-5 psychedelic mushroom experience, and has become spiritually wealthy (gained spiritual knowledge), and seen the truth about "the world". At this level most people are gripped by fear of leaving the world, because what lies beyond is difficult to understand, and we always fear what we don't understand. In order to become fully spiritually conscious, one needs learn how to push past the fear in order to completely separate, and let go (renounce) of everything in "the world". This is what magic mushrooms help you learn.

111. Jesus said, "The heavens and the earth will roll up in your presence, and whoever is living from the living one will not see death."

This refers to a level 5 psychedelic mushroom experience, in which a complete separation from this physical reality is experienced and one becomes in unity with God (living from the living one), although even a level 5 experience is only temporary, the spiritual knowledge you gain from it cannot be dismissed or forgotten, and the fear of permanent physical death disappears (therefore you will not see or taste it) Ultimately during a level 5 psychedelic mushroom experience, you will realize that you are not dying, you are only waking up.

Does not Jesus say, "Those who have found themselves, of them the world is not worthy"?

This refers to one who has used the magic mushroom to attain spiritual consciousness (gone to heaven) (found themselves) but returned to "the world" (returned to hell, spiritual unconsciousness) for the sake of helping others find their own spiritual consciousness.

112. Jesus said, "Damn the flesh that depends on the soul. Damn the soul that depends on the flesh."

This refers to our evil physical bodies with all of their insatiable desires and how our spirits provide the energy for them to work. The flesh is evil and in turn the soul that gives in (surrenders control, becomes a slave) to the flesh's evil insatiable physical desires (the pleasures of the flesh) is damned to suffer its fate (death). By eating the "manna" (psilocybin mushrooms) you are seeking to learn how to let go of the flesh.

113. His disciples said to him, "When will the kingdom come?"

"It will not come by watching for it. It will not be said, 'Look here!' or 'Look, there!' Rather, the Father's kingdom is spread out upon the earth, and people don't see it."

This refers to magic mushrooms being the keys to finding the way to heaven, and how they grow all over the earth, but due to the fact that the church has hidden the truth about them by changing the name and the image, and deeming them forbidden, people don't see them as they truly are". We must all seek it out to learn it (experience it) for ourselves, no physical person can take you to (or show you) the kingdom of heaven (spiritual consciousness) because the kingdom of heaven is within each of us. Magic mushrooms make us able to understand this. Eat magic mushrooms and have a "level 5" psychedelic experience to understand.

114. Simon Peter said to them, "Make Mary leave us, for females don't deserve life".

Jesus said, "Look, I will guide her to make her male, so that she too may become a living spirit resembling you males. For every female who makes herself male will enter the kingdom of Heaven".

This refers to the idea that physical women are evil because they seek the attention of males and by drawing the attention of males, they draw males down a physical path. Women were created by the Demiurge to be attractive to males so that physical offspring could be produced in order to further the demiurges plan. Women seek to control the thoughts of men through the use of physical desire. Men who are impure with physical desire are easy for them to distract. Once one uses the magic mushroom, they begin to become strong against physical desire. Those women, who use the "manna" (psilocybin mushroom) to overcome their desire for attention and to bear children and instead put on the mindset of a spiritual guide instead of a physical distraction, can also attain spiritual perfection.

Everyone regardless of the differences between male and female are capable of overcoming their physical natures and desires. There is no difference between male and female in the eyes of God. This is easily understood after eating magic mushrooms.

CHAPTER 3

HOW TO GROW YOUR OWN PURIFIED PSILOCYBIN MUSHROOMS

Okay, I intend to keep this section a short as possible in order to keep it as simple as possible. I'm just going to teach you the best way that I have found to grow them with the lowest possible percentage of failure. This way is a bit more expensive than the budget minded version documented in "the magic mushroom growers guide", but it more than pays for the initial investment with the amount of ease of maintenance during the "fruiting" phase, and the sheer amount of fruits this method produces. If you want to find the cheaper and more labor intensive version, it can be found and printed for free by simply looking up "The magic mushroom growers guide" on the internet.

Now, for a list of the supplies you will need:

- Large bag of medium ground Vermiculite
- Package of "health food store" organic brown rice flour
- Gallon jug of distilled water
- Three large deep foil pans
- 6 or 8 quart pressure cooker
- Ultra sonic "cool mist" humidifier
- Two Styrofoam coolers
- Sheet of Plexiglas
- Tube of silicone
- Two wire mesh pencil trays to fit in bottom of cooler
- Box of 5 gallon zip lock bags
- Box of gallon zip lock bags

- Roll of "breathable" cloth tape
- Two dozen ½ pint mason jars
- One foil cookie sheet
- A fine wire mesh to fit over the cookie sheet
- Two small rolls of 3/8 clear vinyl tube
- Package of 3/8 grommets
- Three empty 2 liter bottles
- Small fluorescent tube lamp, blue white bulb
- Three psilocybin cubensis spore syringes (I prefer the "Orissa" strain for two reasons)

The "Orissa" strain is good for its large growth size and potency, and it was also originally discovered along the banks of the Narmada river in India (Which is considered one of the most sacred of the holy rivers of India) and Jesus, according to the book "Jesus, The missing years", made a stop in Orissa along his journey to Jerusalem.

The initial investment to setup your grow system will be approximately 200-250$ (including the purchasing of your spore syringes). Many of the items on the list can be found at the local "mart" store. You will have to go to a hardware store for a few of the items. The vermiculite was one of the hardest things for me to find, but I ended up finding it at a wholesale landscaping supply store.

The initial effort to get started is a bit overwhelming, but once you have your own "level 5" experience and reach the most major turning point in your life, you will know, the end definitely justifies the means.

Okay, the first step is preparing your substrate. Substrate is the sterilized medium that your spores will colonize and your psilocybin mushrooms will grow on. In order to prepare your substrate you will need to combine 2/3 cup of vermiculite, ¼ cup of organic brown rice flour, and ¼ cup of distilled water in a bowl for each ½ pint jar you intend to prepare. I always mix my mixture in bulk, usually a large bowl with enough of each ingredient for about 8-10, ½ pint jars. For a little added sterility I like to place my brown rice flour and vermiculite in their own separate deep foil pans and place them in the oven at 300 degrees for about 30 minutes, and boil my distilled water for 15 minutes before combining the measured amounts. Sterility is the key to success. Keep your preparation area clean. Contamination will stop you in your tracks. Mixing the ingredients in bulk is physically demanding, (your arm will get tired) I use a butter knife to stir with to make it easier.

Once you've mixed the pre-measured amounts of ingredients together to form something that looks similar to thick, damp, oatmeal, you are ready to fill your jars. One very important step is to poke four holes in the lid at four corners of the sealing portion of the lid. The holes are made for two important reasons, first, you need a way to inject your spores into the sterilized growing media, and second, the jars will explode if you heat them up without allowing them to release pressure.

Fill the jars to the bottom of the threaded area only and don't pack it too tightly. Little bitty gaps and air pockets in the mixture are good. They actually help the colonization process. Once you've filled the jar to the bottom of the threads with mixture, wipe the threaded area above the mixture completely clean. It has to be spotless, inside and out, or contamination has a higher chance of occurring. After you've cleaned the threaded area completely, then fill the jar the rest of the way with plain dry vermiculite. This layer will provide one of the barriers against invading contamination spores. After you fill it the rest of the way, tighten the lid down onto the jar and cover the lid with a piece of tin foil or two. You use the tinfoil to prevent water from getting into the jars through the holes when you boil the jars.

Once you've prepared enough jars to fill the bottom of the pressure cooker, place two wash cloths in the bottom of the pot in order to prevent the jars from sitting directly on the bottom during the cooking process (or they'll get too hot and crack, or dehydrate, either occurrence means failure). Fill the pot with enough water to come up the side of the Jar ¾ of the way. Don't have the jars floating around but have enough water to heat the jars thoroughly. Boil the Jars for 30 minutes at 10-15 psi in the pressure cooker. Prepare more jars while you are waiting for those to boil thoroughly. After they have cooked sufficiently, take them out of the pot and place two jars in each gallon zip lock bag. Allow the jars to cool overnight in the zip lock bags. Once you've repeated the process until you've either run out of media, or run out of jars, then relax, the real tough part is over. The rest is a cool science experiment.

The next morning after your jars have cooled, have the spore syringes ready to inoculate. (Inoculate is a fancy word for "squirt some of the spore solution out of the needles and into the jar through the hole of the lid on the jar") This is the fun part. Shake the tubes vigorously to insure the spores are well dispersed in the liquid. Don't worry if you cannot see anything in the liquid (good spores are almost impossible to see with the naked eye, and the best results I've gotten so far, came from syringes which I didn't see anything in them except clear liquid). The tubes of solution usually come without the needle attached, so remove the plug/ cap thing from the end and screw the needle on. Take the foil off your first jar and stick the needle all the way into one of the holes in the lid. The hole at the tip of the needle needs to be facing the glass so you can see the hole in the needle from the outside. Squirt about ½ cc. into each hole, as far in as you can, against the side of the jar, for a total of 1 ½ -2 cc.'s per jar. After you've squirted a little solution into each hole and every hole has been inoculated, cover the hole with a piece of "breathable" cloth tape. You do this to prevent bugs (like flies, nats, and ants) and other (bad) spores from easily getting in. Inoculate the rest of the jars you've prepared and repeat the procedure of covering the inoculated holes with breathable tape. Chances are you will lose a couple of jars to contamination but for the most part, if you follow these basic precautionary steps, 90% of your jars will turn out "good-to-go".

After you've inoculated and taped, then put your jars in a warm (the optimum temp range is 75-82 degrees) dark (there must be no light at all, like the cabinets over the fridge or a tool cabinet in the garage) place, and let them do their thing. After a week or two, you should have white patches showing up in many of the jars. Usually 3-4 weeks after the inoculation, your jars should be mostly white (or all white, I've had jars completely "colonized" in 3 weeks).

One very important note: Be on the lookout for any colors that might appear in the jar. Colors (any other than white) are a sign of contamination, and the jar must be thrown out. As long as your jars don't turn funny colors (I've seen, green, pink, black), you should be about ready to take your white "cake" out of the jar. Make sure that the bottom of the jar is completely covered by the white "mycelium" before you try and take it out of the jar. If you try and rush it, your "cake" will become contaminated and all your hard work and waiting will be for nothing. In fact, it is better to wait a week or two after the "cake" has been completely covered by the white "mycelium". This way the colonized cake's nutrient network is more complete and it will be easier for the "cake" to gain access to the nutrients required to "fruit". (I've had explosions of mushrooms [massive initial flushes] by simply waiting a couple of extra weeks, and struggled when I tried to rush the process, so learn to be patient).

Make sure that before you go opening the jar, you have a terrarium up and running. In order for your completely white "cakes" to begin the "fruiting" process, they require two main things, constant humidity (above 85%, but not 100%) and some light (bright white or "arctic" white light is best). The terrarium helps you accomplish this perfect environment.

Take the Styrofoam coolers and cut a large window in each of the lids. Do it with the lids on the coolers to support the rim of the lid and avoid breakage. Leave a ledge big enough to support the Plexiglas window from underneath. Measure out a square of Plexiglas that is big enough to fit in the lid and silicone it to the supporting ledge of the lid so that when the lid is on the cooler, it seals well. This is your terrarium. Next you need to set up the humidifier. The outlet hole in the humidifier tank is too large, so you'll have to plug it (I closed mine and just drilled a new hole). I used some duct tape to seal off the gaps at the edge of the outlet area to make sure all my humidity goes out through my newly drilled hole. The humidifier pumps out too much humidity, even at the lowest setting, so a set of drying chambers is necessary. This step is easier than it sounds. See the picture for an example.

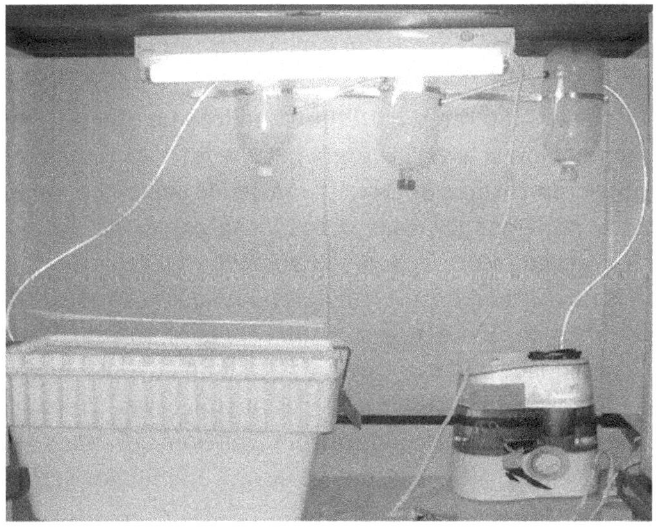

Take your three 2 liter bottles, turn them so that the cap faces down and drill a hole (try and make the hole as "clean" as possible for the best seal of the tube and grommet) in the side near the top that used to be the bottom. Exactly on the other side of the bottle drill another hole, halfway down the side. Repeat the process for each bottle. Take a grommet and insert it into each hole. Cut lengths of the clear vinyl tubing and connect the humidifier to the bottles, and the bottles to the bottles. Inlet should be the highest hole and outlet should be the lower one. There should be no low spots in the tubing or they'll clog up with water and it will prevent humidity from getting into the terrarium. After connecting the bottles, cut one more length of tubing to connect the last bottle to the terrarium. Drill a hole in the upper corner of the terrarium to insert the tubing into the terrarium. Fill your humidifier (don't use the demineralization cartridge) and turn it on. After a few minutes, you should see a small amount of fog coming out of the tube leading into the terrarium. I like to use a cheap thermometer/humidity gauge in my terrarium so that I can tell at a glance how the environment is without disturbing anything. Put the metal mesh screen in the bottom of the terrarium to keep the cakes off of the bottom of the terrarium and let it run for a little while longer. You want to make sure everything is functioning properly so you don't kill any cakes.

Once you are sure that your terrarium is operating well enough to maintain a constant 80-90% humidity level and a 70-80 degree temperature range, and you have a light set up that reaches the bottom of the terrarium through the Plexiglas window, then you're ready to begin the fruiting stage.

Open the jars which have been fully colonized for at least a week or more. Gently shake off the dry vermiculite on the top of the cake. Don't pick at it, just gently tap the side of the jar to free up the part that remains loose and gently blow it away. Loosely put the lid back on the jar and turn it over. Lightly tap the jar on your hand to dislodge the cake from the bottom of the jar. Once the cake drops loosely onto the lid, gently twist the jar until it lets go of the lid and you are able to remove the jar from the cake which is now sitting upside down on the lid. Try to touch the cake as little as possible. I place one finger in the very center of the bottom of the cake to hold it in place and flip it over as I sit it on its' bottom on the metal mesh grate. Repeat this process for as many cakes as you intend to "birth". A regular size Styrofoam terrarium will hold 6-8 cakes with enough room to "fruit" abundantly and the ultrasonic humidifier setup can keep up with as many mushrooms as the cakes can grow at any time.

It can take anywhere from 3-10 days for little mushrooms to form. You need to keep the water in the humidifier full and fresh, and the cakes need at least 2 hours of light everyday (I give my cakes 12 hours of light a day). Keep an eye on the tubes which connect the 2 liter bottles to make sure they don't get clogged and empty the 2 liter bottles frequently. Overall this system requires about 15 minutes of attention a day. The first indicator of growth you will see is that the mycelium will become fluffy and begin to resemble hoarfrost (see the covers). Soon after that you will notice small, dark brownish-red, round balls seemingly appearing out of thin air in just the hint of moisture or "dew" that has formed on the mycelium. Seeing those little round balls for the first time is a feeling that's hard to describe. It's something special you'll just have to experience for yourself.

Once the little mushrooms begin to form, they will be ready to pick after about 5-8 days. They grow incredibly fast, doubling or tripling in size every day. You know they are ready to pick when the larger, golden brown ball on the end of the stick tears away at the bottom and it takes on the appearance of a little umbrella.

Once you're ready to begin picking mushrooms, you need to think about how to preserve them. Rarely will you have enough mushrooms become ready for a full dose when fresh. One of the only ways to preserve them in an edible state is to dry them out. You cannot use heat to dry them though. The best way to dry them is to use some desiccant (you get it in the "paint" section at the hardware/ home improvement store) in a foil cake pan suspended above another deeper pan, with another screen suspended about 1" over the desiccant. Place the fresh mushrooms on the grate over the desiccant, careful not to let the desiccant touch the mushrooms. Tape the foil pans to the wire mesh grate to stabilize the dryer setup, and then put the entire setup inside the 5 gallon zip lock bag and lock it. In a day or two they will be dry enough to store without spoiling and they will be every bit as potent as if they were fresh.

That is basically it, with a bit of fortitude and effort, you will have your own little spiritual communion garden capable of growing the fruit which God gave us all for the sole purpose of reconnecting our spiritual selves and minds to him and can ultimately return us all to our spiritual consciousness.

Remember, you enter the bridal suite with God with a 5 dried gram level dose. I cannot begin to tell you how important it is that you keep your mind open to this truth that I've given you here. Ultimately, it's your eternal life that depends on what you do with this book. For your sake, I hope you try it for yourself to see whether or not it's true. If you do try it and want to tell me thanks, just tell your friends, that's all the thanks I want, (to complete the task put before me) and if you dismiss this truth and continue "walking by faith" (brainwashed by "the church")alone, don't say that I didn't warn you, or nobody tried to tell you! It is time for us all to wake up! – Sean Williams (808)554-1496 (my cell # just in case you want to talk)

We are all born with the ability to transcend our physical form and go to heaven, but just like anything else, it is a learned ability. Transcendence is the shift from one's physical consciousness to the spiritual consciousness. This is what magic mushrooms do. They show us temporarily what our spiritual consciousness (heaven) is like, so that when the end of our physical life comes, we are ready for it and accept it, instead of being afraid of it and getting stuck here.

If you still don't believe in what I've tried to tell you, at least use the Wikipedia, to do your own research into mysticism, psychedelic experience, near death experience, psilocybin mushrooms, war in heaven, final judgment, plan of salvation, reincarnation, catharism, consciousness and hell. Maybe then you will begin to understand that the original "fallen" angels only "fell" unconscious in heaven as they came into the physical world, and as we are all born of them, we are all born in the same unconscious state. We just simply need to learn how to "wake up".

Good luck to you my brothers and sisters, I hope this book has helped you....

This ying-yang symbol shows us a life journey. We all start in the darkness, with just the smallest amount of light within us. Through the use of the true fruit of knowledge and constant effort to stay on the spiritual path, we can begin the shift. By overcoming our physical selves, we can overcome the darkness, grow spiritually and become beings of light. This symbol represents who you are inside your skin. Once the black dot in the white is gone, you're home.

www.ingramcontent.com/pod-product-compliance
Lightning Source LLC
Chambersburg PA
CBHW030157070426
42447CB00031B/835

* 9 7 8 0 5 7 8 0 3 1 9 9 6 *